75p

THE CIVIL SERVANT AND
HIS WORLD

IN THE SAME SERIES

THE ARTIST AND HIS WORLD
by Julian Trevelyan

THE NURSE AND HER WORLD
by Pamela Bright

THE TEACHER AND HIS WORLD
by Walter James

THE LAWYER AND HIS WORLD
by Ewan Mitchell

THE PROBATION OFFICER AND HIS
WORLD
by Marjory Todd

THE MUSICIAN AND HIS WORLD
by Lionel Salter

THE FILM-MAKER AND HIS WORLD
by R. J. Minney

THE DOCTOR AND HIS WORLD
by J. G. Thwaites

THE ACTOR AND HIS WORLD
by Dulcie Gray and Michael Denison

DANCERS AND THEIR WORLD
by Susan Lester

CHILD CARE OFFICERS
AND THEIR WORLD
by John Stroud

THE DENTIST AND HIS WORLD
by Leslie J. Godden

THE CIVIL SERVANT AND HIS WORLD

by

JOHN CARSWELL

LONDON
VICTOR GOLLANCZ LTD
1966

© JOHN CARSWELL 1966

'To become a *kwan* (Chinese official) it is necessary to be morally sound, honest, upright, and enlightened (*tsin, tmen, lyen, min*). If persons possessing these qualities are not available, a selection is made from among others.'

MADE AND PRINTED IN GREAT BRITAIN BY
THE GARDEN CITY PRESS LIMITED
LETCHWORTH, HERTFORDSHIRE

CONTENTS

	Introduction	7
I	What is a Civil Servant?	11
II	The Shape of the Civil Service	22
III	Civil Service History and Tradition	39
IV	Generalizers	50
V	Specialists and Scientists	64
VI	Recruitment and Conditions of Service	78
VII	Red Tape: A Civil Servant's Work	92
VIII	Atmosphere and Manners	106
IX	Out of the Office	117
X	Conclusion: Credits and Debits	126

Appendices

A	List of Government Departments	139
B	Entry to the Civil Service	142
C	Short List for Further Reading	144

INTRODUCTION

In this short book about the Civil Service I have tried to see the Civil Service as a whole, and where I have entered into detail it has only been by way of illustration. I have not gone in for constitutional or any other kind of theory. The book is impressionistic: neither exact nor deep. It is intended to give a picture of a necessary, interesting, and developing profession, about which much is said, but little is understood.

The book represents my own views, and I suppose must reflect my own experience. Other civil servants would have written differently. I have had the help and advice of a few friends and colleagues, but the responsibility for what I say is mine and mine alone.

Writing it has shown me how difficult it is to take an objective view of one's own profession. There is nothing like leather to a shoemaker. What I have tried to avoid is cosiness (the Civil Service is far from snug, if it ever was); an impression of 'effortless superiority' (I have seen it achieved, but it is no longer the important thing); and excessive technicality. But I have referred to some technicalities, because the idea that administration is an amateur business is still strong in this country. It is an idea that does great harm to those who think of following administration as a career.

My attempt to be comprehensive has made me conscious of a great many omissions. I would have liked, for instance, to have said rather more about the relationship between the

Civil Service and Parliament, but did not want to devote too much of my space to the comparatively small part of the Civil Service which comes into direct contact with Parliament. The witness's chair at committees of enquiry, and the 'official box' (a queer kind of jury-box just outside the boundaries of each chamber of the legislature, in which civil servants sit during debates and prepare notes for the Minister dealing with the debate) play a large part in some civil service careers. But there are few countries where the distinction between officials and the elected is more firmly established than this one: the notion that an official, however senior, should speak in a Parliamentary committee to explain even the most technical point in a measure which is under consideration, is abhorrent to every principle on which parliamentary business is conducted. The effect of this is to compel Ministers to master detail. The civil servant, in this country, is never an advocate.

And yet heads will still wag and say 'we know quite well, for all this modesty, that civil servants really run the country'. It is true that without a civil service the country could not be run. But that is not the same as saying civil servants run it— any more than waiters run a restaurant, though without them the restaurant could not be run. On the whole the civil servant does not make choices: he presents them in analytic form. He does not make precedents: he applies them. He does not create events: he reacts effectively to them. He does not decide what the future will hold: he works out what is probable on different assumptions. In civil service life, as in other kinds of life, what has to be done is often the only thing there is to do, but it takes a certain amount of thought to decide what it is. The seeker for direct power would be ill advised to choose the Civil Service as a career.

It is not the making of decisions, but the making of new ideas, that provides the deepest satisfaction for civil servants. Invention, innovation, even extemporization, are the real demands on the mind. It is said that during the war a highly placed official volunteered to spend his leave doing work on the land. He was sent by the farmer to sort a mound of potatoes into large potatoes and small. After two hours he was found sitting in front of two small heaps, one consisting of huge potatoes, the other of tiny ones, with a middle-sized potato in his hand. He was saying 'These decisions! I must make a sieve.'

It has been said that the civil servant has an objection to every solution, and it is probably true that he sees the disadvantages in anything more quickly than the advantages. By training and habit he is a critic and a conscience. It is his job to analyse consequences and point them out. The most serious professional sin of a civil servant is to flatter what he is asked to consider. In technical terminology, it is far graver to underestimate cost than to overestimate: a good financial official is far more likely to say 'this will cost you more than you think, so you must have less of it', than 'this costs too much'.

No doubt the permanence of the Civil Service gives a stability to the state which it would not have otherwise. But the shape and outlook of the Civil Service must change with society, and it is clear to me that very great changes will take place in the Civil Service in coming years. What they will be I do not know. But the more fully stretched a society is—and it seems to me that our society will be more and more fully stretched—the more administration it seems to require. The last war, I suppose, demanded more tautness in the use of resources than any period before or since. It also—despite the needs of the forces and the factories—demanded a larger, and more overburdened civil service.

Coming years are likely to repeat this pattern. Severe demands will be made on every side for skilled manpower and womanpower. Yet the tasks of the Civil Service and the demand for administrators to deal with the complexities of modern society will continue to grow.

CHAPTER I

WHAT IS A CIVIL SERVANT?

WHAT IS A civil servant? In a way the very question
implies that a civil servant is writing this book, because most
people have very little doubt about the answer. But perhaps
even the most positive person would find the answer not quite
so easy to put into words as his reply, say, to 'what is a doctor,
or a teacher, or a musician?' These are professions which
have at their core some particular skill devoted to a particular
objective. The doctor's training is designed to answer the over-
riding purpose of his career—the treatment and cure of our
ailments. His professional morality, his outlook on life, his
social relationships, all flow from this.

Some doctors are also civil servants—the Chief Medical
Officer of the Ministry of Health, for instance, or the doctors
who advise on war pension and industrial injury claims: and
the fact that one can be both tells something about the difference between the two professions. Some teachers are civil
servants—indeed in many countries *all* teachers, including
university professors, are civil servants. The Civil Service even
contains some musicians. It is impossible to name a profession
which is not represented in the Civil Service: scientists of
every kind, engineers, architects, quantity surveyors, lawyers,
actuaries, accountants, journalists.

At the other extreme there are great numbers of civil servants working in ways that are common to all big organizations: typists, clerks, telephone operators, liftmen and
printers. The managers and the barmaids in the pubs of

Carlisle are civil servants, and so are the staff of the Victoria and Albert Museum. Other civil servants are concerned with the working of services—large or small—which are directly operated by the state : postmen, for instance, and the Warders (wrongly called Beefeaters) in the Tower of London.

But one does not think of the doctor who deals with one's war pension or the man who draws half a pint of bitter in a Carlisle pub as a civil servant. And very few of us would be content with a definition of a civil servant as a person who works for the community, and not on his own account. In a sense we all work for the community, and some of us who do so are not civil servants on any reckoning. Judges, for instance, are not (what a row there would be if it were suggested they should be), nor are policemen (except Defence Department policemen). Most teachers, the whole National Health Service, and the whole of Local Government, are outside the Civil Service. So of course, are politicians.

Must we then, in despair, say that being a civil servant is just a legal, technical question, the arbitrary result of rules and history? If so, there would be little point in writing this book. Just as a point has no magnitude, people with a merely technical position have no world. A book about such a Civil Service would have no design one could point to. It would be just a list of jobs to which certain conditions of service were attached.

This would not only be dreary. It would deny the idea—solid but imprecise—that comes into the ordinary person's mind when the words 'civil servant' are uttered. This idea cuts through all these complications I have been talking about, with their contrasts between professionalism and legal status, and relates to a person who is concerned, in one way or another, with the central government administration. Concerned, I mean, not with general ideas, but in the context of what is actually happening. Whatever a civil servant's Department, and whatever his rank, he is dealing with real situations not theoretical problems; and he does so with the guidance of a policy which he may help to form but which is none the less binding on him.

The nearest comparison of a physical kind to the Civil Service is perhaps a railway system. The correspondence of the trains with the time-table; the safety of the passengers; the continuity; the complexity; and above all the sense that each railwayman has a responsibility to the system as a whole as well as to the performance of his own particular task—all these have their comparison in the Civil Service. The goods porter will notice—should notice—that a red lamp is missing from the rear coach of an express as it passes through his way-side station, and report it. The Civil Service principal will notice—should notice—a slip of fact in the draft of a memorandum prepared by the Permanent Secretary for the Minister. It is not my object to be idyllic about the Civil Service; and it is very important not to be so, for two reasons. Firstly, the work of many civil servants—apart from the civil service flavour of all being in it together, which I am trying to convey—is not really very different from the sort of work people do in many other large organizations. Even administration, which I suppose most people think of as the typical civil servant's job, is not peculiar to Government. Goodness only knows it is needed in industry, in business, in almost any co-ordinated human activity. It consists, fundamentally in making suitable arrangements to further whatever is in hand. Women running households exercise many of the administrator's skills.

The second reason is that the Civil Service is not only subject to change—all professions would claim to be this—but is not master of the changes it undergoes. There are, of course, trends of opinion in the Civil Service itself about how it should develop and adapt to a changing world. Many of these opinions find their outlet through the various professional associations of civil servants, and others are the deeply held convictions of individuals. But none are decisive, or even very influential, for the way the Civil Service develops. The demands of society itself determine the changing shape and atmosphere of the Civil Service. The members of the Service—like people in other lines of business—may be convinced that the old ways are best : they must change with the times just the same. They have not the alternative of going out of business, like people in private life. The main feature of government (and the Civil Service is the four-fifths of the government iceberg below the waterline) is that by its very nature it cannot go out of business. This has its advantages; but it also means continuous change.

It is quite certain, then, that anyone entering the Civil Service today will see very great alterations to it during his career. This book can give a pattern of the Service as it exists (even this is difficult) and can try to bring out some of the underlying things about civil service life which, in the author's view, seem likely to persist. But whatever eternal truths there may be about the Civil Service the most important of them is that the civil servant should be adaptable, and avoid the cardinal official sin of trying to enforce drills he has learned, regardless of their relevance. It is bad administration, and a source of personal unhappiness to anyone who attempts it.

So those who say civil servants are our masters—a mysterious 'them' who are both inaccessible and capricious—are wrong. The civil servant, according to his position, exercises power and is concerned in decisions which may be important to great numbers of people. Obvious examples are officials concerned with town planning or pensions claims; but the important thing—the thing that governs his whole profession —is that his decisions must match. The same kind of decision on the same kind of case must be given in Camborne and Runcorn. The skill of the civil servant is in transmitting power, not in generating it.

This is really another way of saying that the authority of the civil servant is delegated, and not personal. The decisions he makes aim to be correct in the framework for which the power has been conferred. The commonest reason for friction between a civil servant and the public is not abuse of power but lack of power to make an exception.

This possession of a power that is delegated is what makes the civil servant proverbially cautious. Just because in the ordinary way he will *not* have to take the full rap for a mistaken or unfortunate decision, he avoids risks. It may be unpleasant to reap the results of one's own errors in loss of business or reputation. It is still more unpleasant to have been concerned in a decision which affects the reputation of someone else. Gambling with one's own money may be silly. Gambling with other people's money is wrong.

The person who wants to have a direct and visible influence on public events would be wrong to choose the Civil Service as a career. With patience a civil servant may find himself in a position to shape some piece of legislation or administrative arrangement and be its genuine, but anonymous, author. Pieces of work like this can last for many decades, but only a few people, probably, will ever know that 'this was so and so's idea—he put it through'. Very rarely—as with P.A.Y.E. —does the authorship become known.

The business of a civil servant then, whether it consists of paying the right amount of pension to a given person or advising the Chancellor of the Exchequer on his Budget, is done as part of an organization. This does not mean that civil servants are less colourful than other people—some of them are passionate, some are eccentric. The idea of a civil service 'type' hardly corresponds to reality. But there is a civil service style, set up by this common bond.

The common bond affects most strongly the civil servants who are nearest the centre of affairs. Do not misunderstand me. I do not mean, necessarily, the higher, not the lower ranks. It is as strongly felt, say, by the filing clerks in a Minister's Private Office, or by the security printers who must produce, overnight, some Parliamentary Paper of high importance, as by officials of exalted rank and delicate, far-reaching responsibilities. But at any moment the apparently dim spark of the most remote and routine office may be puffed into glowing embers by some sudden draught down the corridors of power.

So it would give a very imperfect idea of civil service life at any level, or in any speciality, if particular groups were ignored. Though immensely large and complex, the Civil Service is a whole. And although an attempt to explain every one of its ramifications would go far beyond the limits of this book, they must at any rate be sketched if civil service life is to be adequately understood. It will, I hope, be possible to do this, and yet concentrate most on those groups which the general reader thinks of as typically 'civil servants'.

These are the administrative and executive and corresponding 'Departmental' grades; the Scientific Civil Service; and the professional advisers, primarily but by no means only, doctors and lawyers, with whom the run-of-the-mill civil servant is almost certain to come into contact in the course of his or her career. I shall be able to devote less space to the rest of the professional civil service, though the purposes for which the Government employs actuaries, engineers, architects, and many other kinds of professional man is important even for those who do not work in Departments where these skills are directly used.

Except for the Stationery Office, which is a vital part of the Civil Service as a whole, I shall not deal with what is known as the Industrial Civil Service—e.g. those who work in Government-owned factories. Nor, although the presence of the Post Office down to the most remote village counter is an essential part of Government, shall I have much to say about postmen and telephone operators (who are civil servants) or village sub-postmistresses (who are not).

I shall make one other large exclusion. It is an arbitrary one, but I think it is justified by the general idea of a civil servant as a home-based person. Life in an office whose *main* interests are concentrated abroad, and whose staff, as a matter of course, spend a good part of their careers in overseas posts, has special features : knowledge of languages, the protocol of diplomacy, the direct administration of colonial territories, problems of family life overseas : all these come into a career in the Foreign Office, the Colonial Office, or the Commonwealth Relations Office as major matters.

Many civil servants other than those in these offices, of course, go abroad for longer or shorter spells, and readiness to do so is part of the job. So I have said something of this aspect of civil service life, which in some Departments (such as the Board of Trade, the Ministry of Labour, and the Post Office) is an important one, even though the main interest of those Departments is domestic. All that has been left out, therefore, are the particular features that distinguish life in the Overseas Services from civil service life in general.

Even with these exclusions I am left with a very large and diverse field to cover, with many different kinds of life in it : the desk-worker's in Whitehall or elsewhere; the scientist's in a research station : the manager's, the inspector's, the instructor's. They are all bound together by the bond I have mentioned and by two other things.

First, all career civil servants are selected, normally by competition, through the Civil Service Commission. There is no political-spoils system in the Civil Service, and while this puts no ban on even the declared political views of a civil servant, it does prevent him from publicly and formally supporting a political party. It excludes him from standing for Parliament and from sitting (though exceptions have been made) as a party man on a local authority. Perhaps the most grievous professional offence a civil servant can commit is a public declaration of personal opinion about business with which he is officially concerned. It is bad enough if this happens to be opposed to the Government's official position : it can be just as bad if it happens to coincide with it.

The second is that civil servants in this country have, as such, no legal status whatever. There is a paradox here. In practice an established civil servant has about as firm a tenure as any employee could well have : some would say too firm. And yet he has no contract with his employer, no legal right to his salary, no ground for action if his services are instantly dispensed with. In a way this wholly informal relationship between the State and its servants makes the link between them harder, not easier, to break. Where there has been no marriage, the formalities of divorce are also excluded. But this informality also represents a kind of jealousy. One has only to consider the reaction of Parliament and public to an Act creating a statutory right of civil servants to their jobs, to understand what this jealousy is.

This informality about the civil servant's position has important effects on official life. As I have said, it makes him cautious, for the powers he is exercising are not his own. It also makes him informal himself, at any rate so far as the manner of his work is concerned. The formal official act, beloved of the text-book official, is regarded as a tedious technicality by the English civil servant. The affixing of a seal or a signature to an official document is at best the conclusion of the real work; which has consisted of the scribing of minutes containing 'cockshies' or 'comments'; extempore conversations in a colleague's room or on the telephone; more formal meetings; and the patient elaboration and circulation of a text. The process may take months, weeks, days, or only a few hours to complete.

In such an enterprise, of which there are many hundreds, large or smaller, more or less important, in progress at any one time in Whitehall, there may be only two or three civil servants engaged directly. There may be dozens, or even scores. Some will be administrators, others may be experts of different kinds. Each participant will be linked with the other interests and expertise of the Department in which he works.

I once worked as an assessor for my Department on a major committee consisting of eminent people from outside the civil service. An assessor, incidentally, is an official who sits with an independent committee and takes part in their discussions so far as concerns his Department's business, but has no voice as a member of the committee. This particular committee sat for two years collecting the information they wanted, sifting the evidence, and composing their report. When the day came for the report to be published a party was given at the expense of the members of the committee* for all those, up and down Whitehall, who had helped the committee in one way or another. It was found that even

---

* I might well have been criticized if I had not made this clear. Civil servants are fond of parties, but usually pay for them themselves.

after cutting out those whose contribution was judged too slight, the guests came to well over a hundred. If every official who had at any time checked a fact, weighed an opinion, typed, duplicated, or otherwise helped to process the committee's material had been included, the number might have been five times as great.

While in some ways, the atmosphere in which many civil servants work resembles what one finds in other kinds of business, there are important differences. The public nature of the Civil Service requires that the salary of every civil servant should be generally known. As a result every civil servant knows where every other civil servant stands as regards money from the firm. This undoubtedly contributes to solidarity and confidence in colleagues. Jealousies and uncertainties are reduced to the minimum.

On the whole the Civil Service is still considered as a life career in this country. There is security for the public in this, as well as for the civil servant. However upright the civil servant may be, there are obvious disadvantages to the public in allowing him to be released too easily into jobs where his skill and know-how about the workings of government are turned to the private advantage of his new employers. There are strong arguments on the other side as well, and the picture may change. Even now many civil servants make second careers for themselves with their civil service pension rights intact; and more will undoubtedly do so in future. But there can be no doubt that the tone today is still set by the idea of commitment to a full career.

But whether it is for a life career or not, the fashionable word 'commitment' does undoubtedly apply to the civil servant. He does not just work for the Government: in a very real sense he (or she) is part of the Government, and as such shoulders a fragment of responsibility in governing. Awareness of this responsibility is what gives shape to the civil servant's world: this, and the fascination of watching some corner or other of the never ending and irreversible progress of history develop. With all its frustrations and its anonymity so far as the public is concerned, the life of a civil servant is concerned with the real world and with life as it is lived; not with non-events and manufactured personalities.

CHAPTER II

THE SHAPE OF THE CIVIL SERVICE

THERE ARE SEVERAL ways of describing the general shape of an organization so complex and widespread as the Civil Service—several ways of seeing it as a whole. One can list the various Departments, and group them together by their field of work or the sorts of civil servants that work in them. Or one can describe how the civil servants themselves are distributed geographically, what numbers there are in each class and each rank, and how many are men, and how many are women.

To begin with total numbers: the non-industrial Civil Service (i.e. excluding those doing industrial work in such establishments as Admiralty Dockyards) consists of nearly three-quarters of a million people. Of these about 220,000 are postmen, sorters, telephone operators, and engineers who keep the Post Office going. The rest, in 1963, were divided like this between the broad classes:

Administrative class	2,573
Executive class	74,002
Inspectorates	2,722
Professional, Scientific, and Technical	77,299
Ancillary Technical	49,248
Clerical	196,983
Typists	27,474
Messengers, Porters, &c.	33,963

Of these about 340,000 were permanent, the rest were

temporary. Of the temporary about half were in the clerical and typing grades.

The distribution of the Service over the country is not what most people think. The Post Office, of course, has to spread its staff roughly in accordance with the population. But even apart from this, well over half the civil service works outside London, and this proportion is growing. It is Government policy that as much civil service work as possible should be done outside London, and, indeed, outside the congested South East. About 8 per cent of all civil servants employed by 'home' departments work in Scotland, just under 4 per cent in Wales, and about $2\frac{1}{2}$ per cent overseas, including Northern Ireland. The provinces in England today probably claim about half the Civil Service. The rest—about a third— is in London.

When one comes to look at the kinds of work that are done in the provinces and in London, certain differences at once appear. The work of the administrative class, which is closely tied to Parliament and the Cabinet, is necessarily concentrated on the capital, and the only really big group of administrative civil servants outside London is the staff of the four Scottish Departments forming Edinburgh's Whitehall, St. Andrew's House. But nowadays there are an increasing number of administrative class posts outside London. There is an important group at Cardiff (where a Welsh name, and preferably a knowledge of Welsh, is a consideration); the new regional network of the Department of Economic Affairs includes a number of under-secretary posts; and the senior regional officers of the social service Departments—e.g. the Ministry of Labour—are often assistant secretaries. It will be increasingly common for an administrator in a social service or economic Department to spend part of his career out of London, just as it has long been a feature of a career in a

Department with overseas connexions such as the Board of Trade, for part of a career to be spent abroad. Much the greater part of the Scientific Civil Service works outside London in the various research stations and specialized laboratories maintained by Government Departments.* The Revenue Departments—Customs, Inland Revenue—must, like the Post Office, deploy their staff roughly in accordance with population, trade and industry. The same is true of the big Social Service Departments—Pensions, Labour, National Assistance Board; and of the Ministry of Public Building and Works. Many other Departments have outstations. For instance a large part of the Ministry of Defence is at Bath, and their major computer, which is also used by the Registrar General, is in Sussex. Even those Departments which have no standing regional organization because the main service with which they are concerned is administered by local authorities (Education is a good example) have inspectors or other officers whose main concern is with a circuit outside London.

Turning now to the people themselves, about two-thirds of the whole civil service is made up of men, and one-third of women. In the clerical and typing grades, as one would expect, there are more women than men. But there are four hundred men typists, and it is probably true to say that there are more women in middle and senior management in the Civil Service (and more men in modest posts) proportionately, than in any other big executive organization in this country. About one executive civil servant in five is a woman, and about one administrator in ten. Several women have reached the headship of a Department, and taking the three highest grades (Secretary, Deputy Secretary, and Under-Secretary), there were in 1963 ten women and 331 men. It is

* See Chapter V.

of some interest that the six women Under-Secretaries at that date were aged between 44 and 54. The span of their male colleagues was from 41 to 65.

The age structures of the various classes are very different, and vary in some cases as between men and women. The administrative and executive classes are typical 'pyramids', or rather 'lozenges', with the main bulk of membership in the middle years between thirty and fifty. But the pattern in the clerical grade is quite different. The main body of men in the clerical grades is in the age-groups 40 to 60, with another large batch in their early twenties. But more than a third of women clerical assistants are 22 or under; and for reasons that can well be understood, there are comparatively few in their late twenties and thirties: the age of homes and babies.

Among the scientists the great majority of graduates are men; but one in seven of the scientific assistants and experimental officers are women, and quite a number of women are in the Senior Experimental Officer and Chief Experimental Officer grades. That a man should work for a woman, and take orders from her, is entirely accepted in the Civil Service, which is more than can be said of many business organizations.

What, speaking very generally, would one expect the ages of the different kinds of civil servant to be? The ranges are always wide, even for Permanent Secretaries, of whom the youngest is likely to be in his later forties, and the eldest in his early sixties. An Assistant Secretary, typically, will be fortyish, and a Principal will be in his middle thirties.* The executive class yields wider ranges than the administrative. Its more senior members are likely to be latish forties and upwards, but there are quite a lot of Chief Executive Officers and above who are barely forty, or are even under that age.

* These ranks are more fully explained in Chapter IV.

The other, and more usual way of looking at the Civil Service as a whole, is to divide it up into groups of departments. There are several ways of doing this: one can take large departments as one group, and small ones as another; or distinguish between those which administer a service directly, those which deal through local authorities, and the others. Or one could take groups each of which is concerned with one broad aspect of government—taxes, social services, and the economy. I propose to adopt the last—though it involves some overlapping—but first a word is needed about the special position of Scotland, Wales and Northern Ireland.

Northern Ireland has its own Parliament and is responsible for most of its internal affairs. It therefore has its own Civil Service, which is quite distinct from the British Civil Service, though the Civil Service Commissioners carry out the competition for both—and indeed candidates for both services sit the same examination. Interchange between the two services can take place, but it is uncommon. A career begun at Stormont (the headquarters of the Northern Irish Civil Service) usually continues there. Certain British Departments, such as the Post Office and the Revenue Departments, operate in Northern Ireland just as they do in Great Britain, so that there are quite a number of British civil servants in Northern Ireland as well as Northern Irish ones.

Scotland has four government departments (Agriculture, Education, Home and Health, and Development) located in Edinburgh. Collectively, with the secretariat at Dover House in Whitehall, these form the Scottish Office, whose head is the Secretary of State for Scotland. Scotland also has its own legal system, and its own Law Officers and parliamentary draftsmen, as well as a number of smaller offices staffed by civil servants in Edinburgh. The staffs of these Edinburgh-based departments do not count as a separate Civil Service, though, as in many other government departments, many people spend an entire career in St. Andrew's House. But there is a good deal of cross-posting between St. Andrew's House and Whitehall.

It would be a great mistake to suppose that the Scottish or Northern Irish civil servant has a narrower scope than his English colleague. On the contrary, although his scale of operations is smaller, he has usually, as an individual, to cover a broader span of subjects. Compared with the more detailed division of labour at Whitehall, the man at Stormont or St. Andrew's House will find himself covering, say, both pay *and* pensions for policemen *and* firemen, and maintaining contact about these subjects with several opposite numbers in London.

Another demand on the scope of the Scottish or Northern Irish official is that he must be familiar not only with the law and practice in his own country—which is often quite different from the English—but also with what is going on in England on his subject-matter, so that he may be able to make any necessary adjustments. The London officials also, in developing any policy, or framing any new rules, always bear in mind the probability that there will be a Scottish and a Northern Irish angle to what they are doing—possibly also a Scottish or Northern Irish suggestion that will help. This liaison between opposite numbers is a constant feature of Civil Service life, and is not only necessary to get consistency : it often brings a new point from the fresh mind. I can remember one instance of an experienced Stormont official spotting a serious inconsistency in a draft set of regulations which his more compartmented Whitehall colleagues had sent him so that he could consider their bearing on Northern Ireland.

The case of Wales has similarities, but is not quite the same.

There is no separate Welsh legal system, but there is a strong national consciousness, and a widely spoken Welsh language. These facts are recognized by the existence of a separate Cabinet Minister for Welsh questions (the Secretary of State for Wales) and by Welsh branches of several Whitehall Departments (e.g. Health and Education), which very often have a special status. Such branches are usually staffed by civil servants with a Welsh background.

England, for Civil Service purposes, is divided into nine regions, known as 'standard regions'. They are:

Northern: Cumberland, Durham, Northumberland, Westmorland, and the North Riding. The normal regional town is Newcastle upon Tyne.

Ridings: East and West Ridings. The normal regional town is Leeds.

North Midland: Derbyshire, Leicestershire, Notts, Northants, Lincolnshire, Rutland. The normal regional town is Nottingham.

Midland: Herefordshire, Shropshire, Staffordshire, Warwickshire and Worcestershire. The normal regional town is Birmingham.

Eastern: Bedfordshire, Cambridge, Essex, Herts, Hunts, Norfolk and Suffolk. The normal regional town is Cambridge.

North-western: Cheshire and Lancashire. The normal regional town is Manchester.

South-western: Cornwall, Devon, Somerset, Wilts and Gloucestershire. The normal regional town is Bristol.

South-eastern: Broadly the Greater London Council area plus Kent, Surrey and Sussex.

Southern: Berkshire, Bucks, Dorset, Hants and Oxfordshire. The normal regional town is Reading.

The main Whitehall departments with substantial regional networks are:

Economic Affairs; Customs; Inland Revenue; Pensions and National Insurance; Public Building and Works; National Assistance Board; Post Office; Board of Trade; Agriculture; Transport; Power; Defence; Labour.

This gives a clue to which Departments are the largest. The following is a very broad classification:

Large (over 10,000): Defence, Post Office, Agriculture, Aviation (a lot of scientists here), Customs, Inland Revenue, Labour, Assistance Board, Pensions, Home Office (including Prisons), Public Buildings and Works.

Middling (between 3,000 and 10,000): Education and Science, Housing and Local Government, County Courts, Ordnance Survey, Stationery Office, Trade, Transport, Health, Technology.

Small (between 1,000 and 3,000): Treasury, Commonwealth Relations, General Register Office,* Forestry Commission, Central Office of Information, Land Registry, Power, Supreme Court, Overseas Development, Scottish Departments.

Very Small (under 1,000) includes Colonies, Foreign Office (in Great Britain), Economic Affairs.

It will be noticed that size of staff has nothing to do with 'news value'. That has to do with the extent of the job. The 'large' departments employ well over five-sevenths of the whole Civil Service. It is interesting that if, as these facts tend to show, the main task of the Civil Service is the collection and redistribution of money so that it may better serve the purposes of the community, this is done at a very low

* Varies in size according to the weight of census work.

handling charge. If the income and outlay of the Budget plus National Insurance is taken as £7,000m. on each side, the total administrative charge per pound collected and disbursed is just over $2\frac{1}{2}$ per cent, taking each civil servant as costing £1,200 a year on average for pay, accommodation, pen and ink.

But I must now turn from size to functional grouping. The customary way of doing this is to make eight groups—Post Office (on its own), Revenue, Defence, Social Services, Trade and Industry, Agency Services, Central Government, and Overseas. But in practice some Departments overlap these groupings—thus the Treasury comes into them all, and Labour is both Trade and Social Service. The following rather different classification (which contains some overlapping) provides a reasonable map of Whitehall :

'Community Departments' : Health, Labour, Pensions, Education and Science, Home Office, Housing and Local Government, Assistance, General Register Office, Scottish Home and Health, Scottish Education.

'Economic Departments' : Economic Affairs, Board of Trade, Technology, Transport, Labour, Power, Agriculture, Scottish Agriculture, Building and Works, Scottish Development, Land and Natural Resources, Overseas Development.

'Overseas Affairs' : Defence, Aviation, Foreign Office, Colonial Office, Overseas Development.

'Fiscal' : Inland Revenue, Customs and Excise, Pensions.

'Common Service' : Building and Works, Stationery Office, Central Statistical Office, Treasury Solicitor, Government Actuary, General Register Office, Exchequer and Audit Office, Central Office of Information, Ordnance Survey, Treasury.

The 'Community Services' are concerned to a very great extent with what has been called 'the Welfare State'. They administer nation-wide social security systems of National Health, National Insurance, Industrial Injuries, War Pensions, Family Allowances, and National Assistance. They work directly or through specially constituted authorities such as Regional Hospital Boards. But they are also responsible for guiding the no less important parts of the social services which are run by elected local authorities. Education is perhaps the most notable of these; but other important ones are housing, police, fire brigades, old people's homes, mental health, and children's services. The Ministry of Housing and Local Government and its Scottish opposite number is responsible for the Government's general relations with local authorities (though not for guidance on all the specific services which those authorities perform), for the organization and efficiency of local government, and for the public housing programme. The Department of Education and Science, besides being responsible for education generally, is the point of contact with the Research Councils (Science, Medicine, Agriculture, Natural Environment, and Social Science) and with the University Grants Committee, which allocates the support given by the Government to the universities. The Ministry of Labour comes into the Community Services group as well as the Economic, as the payer of unemployment benefit (though the money for this comes from the Ministry of Pensions), the national job-finder, and the guardian of safety and welfare in industry.

This catalogue should show how the daily work of one Department will draw it into contact with many others—even in quite different groups. Thus training for industry involves both Labour and Education and Science; the Legal Aid scheme will bring in both the Lord Chancellor's Department and the National Assistance Board.

I have included the Home Office in the 'Community Services' group, since a great many of the things it does fit best there. Unlike most countries we have no Ministry of Justice. We think of the actual administration of justice as something that has almost nothing to do with 'government', though we look to a parliamentary minister to correct any mistakes we feel our independent judicial system may have made. Some of the functions carried out in other countries by a Minister of Justice are the business of small legal departments which are quite separate from the Home Office: the Lord Chancellor's Department deals with the Legal Aid Scheme, the revision of the law, and judicial appointments; the Director of Public Prosecutions with the prosecution of criminals; and the Law Officers' Department with legal advice to the Government. The Home Office has links with this legal machinery, but is not responsible for it. On the other hand it is responsible for a number of things which would not fit into a Ministry of Justice at all, such as civil defence, immigration, and the protection of birds, animals and children.

The Economic Group obviously includes the Department of Economic Affairs, which is concerned not only with the prosperity of the country as a whole, but with regional prosperity as well. The economic aspects of manpower are the business of the Ministry of Labour (and the Department of Education and Science), who face the world of industrial relations, help settle strikes, and administer the law about conditions of work, hours, and in some cases, pay. The Ministries of Transport and Power between them cover the Government's relationships with most of the nationalized industries (Coal, Gas, Electricity, Air Lines and Railways).

The Ministry of Transport is directly responsible for the major road-building programme (which brings it into contact with Local Authorities), and, of course, for road safety—which is a community rather than an economic service.

The Board of Trade is one of the most important economic departments, and has as wide a range as any office in Whitehall. It is the Ministry of both internal and overseas commerce. One large part of its work is tariffs (on which, of course, it works closely with Customs) and our trade relations abroad, including exports. Many of its officers serve overseas for part of their careers. At home encouragement given to private industry through 'advance factories' and industrial estates comes through the Board of Trade. Registration of patents and trade marks, consumer protection, the regulation of companies, the law of copyright, all come under this great umbrella. Apart from the nationalized industries, and industries with a high technological content such as electronics and machine tools, most of the relations between the Government and industry are conducted by the Board of Trade.

The Ministry of Technology is to some extent a missionary department, but it has a number of executive functions as well, mainly in relation to industry. Certain industries such as computers and machine tools are sponsored by the Ministry of Technology, and not the Board of Trade.

The full name of the Ministry of Agriculture is the Ministry of Agriculture, Fisheries, and Food. This not only brings it into relationship with the agricultural and fishing industries, which includes the administration of large subsidies, and veterinary and research services (the Ministry is the largest employer of vets in the country); but also food standards and food hygiene, nutritional surveys of the population, and the control of the price of milk; all of which gives this department a 'community' as well as an 'economic' aspect.

The Ministry of Public Building and Works now ranks as an economic department, and is responsible not only for all building done by the Government, but for the building industry in general. The output of bricks, the development of industrialized building, the general load on the building resources of the country, are all matters on which its Minister can be questioned, as well as the work it does on its own account, which includes parks, palaces, and the preservation of ancient monuments.

With the decline of Empire, there is less emphasis in the Whitehall picture on defence. Until recently there were four separate defence departments, one for each service, and a smaller co-ordinating Ministry of Defence. Now, though the three services remain distinct, they are administered by a single, huge, Department. Alongside it, and as it were handing it the ammunition, is the Ministry of Aviation—which is to a great extent a Ministry of war materials. Although, in some ways, the defence world of Whitehall is more self-contained than the 'community' and 'economic' worlds, it has many contacts with other departments, such as Technology, Public Building and Works, and Education and Science.

This country is (I think) unique in having its external affairs handled by two Departments—the Commonwealth Relations Office and the Foreign Office; but the staff of the two offices are now combined to form a single Diplomatic Service, which mans the embassies and high commissions abroad, as well as the headquarters' offices in London. The Diplomatic Service is outside the scope of this book. Nowadays an increasingly important part of our external relations is played by the Ministry of Overseas Development, which is part of the Home Civil Service, and administers our large programmes of aid to underdeveloped countries. Many of its functions were formerly carried out by the Colonial Office, which is now much smaller than it used to be, but remains responsible for a surprisingly large number of dependent territories, some of which are quite important: Aden, Hong Kong, Gibraltar, British Honduras, the Falkland Islands, and Tonga.

No government is possible without taxation, and an efficient, fair, fiscal system is one of the foundations of civilized society. More revolutions have been precipitated over tax questions than about anything else. In the Fiscal Group of departments the twin pillars are the Customs and the Inland Revenue. Many other departments collect some revenue in the shape of charges or fees, and the Ministry of Pensions and National Insurance, in levying contributions for social security, has some of the characteristics of a revenue department. The Post Office also used to be reckoned a revenue department, and much revenue is still collected through its machinery, but it is now no longer expected to yield a revenue to the State from its own business, and it makes a charge to the other departments for whom it works—even for the 'official paid' envelopes they use.

But the great bulk of taxation is collected through income tax, surtax, corporation tax, and estate duties (*direct* taxes collected by the Inland Revenue); and by *indirect* taxes levied on commodities—purchase tax, duties on alcohol and tobacco, petrol duty, and many others—collected by the Customs. In both these departments investigations and the production of statistics are an important part of the work. Without the statistics produced by the two fiscal departments the management of the economy would not be possible. In addition to its main job of assessing and collecting what is due, the Inland Revenue carries out the valuation of property for all government departments, and for local authorities as the basis for rates.

Finally, the supporting services: I have not tried in this chapter to give a complete list of all the agencies, large and small, which back up the Government's activities in specialized ways and are consequently drawn into many operations which at first sight do not seem to be part of their responsibilities.

The launching of a new government department, or of a Minister with new responsibilities, inevitably involves the Ministry of Works as the Government's universal estate agent, housing manager, and furniture shop.

Every utterance the Government wishes to give to the country or the world is published by the Stationery Office; which, besides being the largest publishing business in Britain, provides all the office supplies the Government needs, from computers to pencil sharpeners. It prints stamps, Acts of Parliament, guides to the Tower of London, and passports. It comes into the life of every government department.

The Central Statistical Office, which forms part of the Cabinet Office, produces the main body of government statistics, known as the Green Book (monthly) and the Red Book (annual digest). This is the core of any plan. The contributions come from many departments, the more important of which have statistical staffs of their own. But it is the job of the C.S.O. to co-ordinate the assumptions on which the various figures are compiled, and eliminate inconsistencies.

The Treasury Solicitor and the Government Actuary are examples of professional advisory services. The Treasury Solicitor (who is also the Queen's Proctor) provides legal advice not only to the Treasury but to all government departments except those which have so much legal business of their own that they are justified in having separate legal divisions. The Government Actuary gives professional advice not only on social security schemes—the indispensable basis for their forward planning—but on many other insurance and pensions matters in which the Government is concerned, including the superannuation of the Civil Service itself, and pensions in the nationalized industries.

Government publicity, about which there are strict rules distinguishing it from political party publicity, is the province of the Central Office of Information, which is also the parent department for the Information Officers of the various departments which have them. Its links throughout Whitehall, and especially with the Stationery Office, are very close, and any Government publicity campaign—say recruitment to the armed forces, the launching of new pension or tax rates, or warnings on road safety, will concern it. It is also the base for the Social Survey—the Government's market research organization.

Finally, in this extremely rapid sketch, I should mention the Exchequer and Audit Department ('E and A' as civil servants usually call it). This office is not often in the public eye, but it is present in every Government Office as the eyes and ears of the Comptroller and Auditor General, who is an officer of Parliament, not of the Government. Its business is the examination and audit of the whole body of official transactions. It serves no Minister. The Comptroller's reports are made to an all-party Committee of Parliament who castigate errors and inefficiency wherever they can be found. The staff of E and A are in most cases stationed in departments carrying on their continuous audit, and are regularly moved round from one job to another.

My purpose in this survey has not been to break up but to throw together the many ingredients that go to the making of Whitehall. On any problem or piece of business which has any importance, several of these ingredients will come rapidly together. It is sometimes said that government departments are jealous of their boundaries, and readily fight one another at the frontiers of their responsibilities. There is a certain truth in this. To operate adequately every civil servant, every branch, and every department, must know where responsibilities begin and end; and it follows that raiders will meet with resistance. Failure to recognize boundaries involves what civil servants call 'crossed wires'; yet sometimes the effective discharge of duty may seem to mean that a boundary ought to be extended.

But what is far more important for an understanding of the Civil Service is the extent and complexity of its interaction. Within 24 hours it can bring together officials, say, from the Ministry of Labour, the Commonwealth Relations Office, the Colonial Office, the Home Office, the Central Office of Information, and the Treasury Solicitor (subject: some aspect of immigration policy); or from the Department of Education and Science, the Ministry of Technology, the Department of Education for Scotland, the Stationery Office, and the Board of Trade (subject: some aspect of computer provision).

The idea that each official, like a mole in his burrow, pursues a narrow allotted task, is the most misleading notion about Whitehall that has ever been propagated. One of the highest skills of a civil servant is the knowledge of how responsibility is distributed, and what skilled resources can— and should—be brought to bear on any problem. A leafing through of the annual *Imperial Calendar and Civil Service List*, which shows in exact detail how the responsibilities of the Government are divided, and how they are affiliated, will tell more than any business directory.

CHAPTER III

CIVIL SERVICE HISTORY AND TRADITION

THE CIVIL SERVICE is so much taken for granted in this country that people assume that it has grown up naturally, like the grass on the Downs or the trees on Hampstead Heath. That this is not the case, can be seen by comparing with the Civil Services of other countries where officials have legal powers, or where advancement in official life depends on political connexions. The Civil Service in this country has, in fact, developed in a highly artificial manner, like a tree pruned and trained against a wall. Some knowledge of this process is needed by anyone who is considering the Civil Service as a career.

Until the last quarter of the eighteenth century there was no systematic civil service. But there were four embryos : the officials who worked on central finance (the Treasury); the group of agencies concerned with defence; the Customs— which until the present century was the only governmental organization except the Post Office to have agencies outside London; and those who worked for the Secretaries of State dealing with internal, external, and colonial affairs.

The Younger Pitt, and the utilitarian reformers who came after him, can be regarded as the founders of the Civil Service as we know it. Their object, which they achieved, was to get rid of the idea that office under the Crown was primarily a way of providing people lucky enough to get it with a salary, and to ensure that where a salary was paid the person

who received it actually worked. It took more than a generation for the old free-holders, who had bought jobs which in
many cases they did not personally perform, to die out. The
age of utilitarian reforms led gradually to an administrative
climax in the changes associated with the names of Macaulay
and Trevelyan.

These changes created the framework of the modern Civil
Service by laying down rules about how officials should be
recruited, and what should be provided for them when they
left. Recruitment was put into the hands of an independent
body called the Civil Service Commission, whose job it was
and is to make sure, with complete impartiality, that those
appointed should be fit for their duties, and (if there are
more candidates than vacancies) that the most fit are
appointed. Hence the absence of any 'spoils system' by which
appointments go to the nominees of those who are in power.

Provision for the termination of an official career, though
less obviously important, was equally vital to the system. A
great defect of the old arrangements was that officials hung on
far too long for efficiency, because they could not afford to
retire; or, still worse, they used their official position to put
something by for the day when they could no longer work. It
is often pointed out that the civil servant, unlike most people,
does not contribute towards his pension. The reason is that the
Civil Service Superannuation Acts, of which the first was in
1834, were based on the idea that the contract between the
state and its servant was for life. At a certain point the
employee would cease to work for the state, but if his service
had been satisfactory he would go on getting a salary.

Although the Trevelyan reforms produced the non-
political civil service recruited by competition which we still
have, another series of changes was needed before the general
organization of the present Civil Service took shape. These

changes belong to the years following the First World War, and are linked with the names of Lord Haldane, Chairman of the Machinery of Government Committee of 1918, and Warren Fisher, who was Permanent Secretary of the Treasury for most of the period between the wars.

The effect of these reforms was to make the staffs of the various departments, which till then had had a great deal of independence and variety, into an integrated service. How one got in in the first place, and what one's pension should be when one retired, had already been settled on a uniform basis; but the organization of what lay between those two dates was not uniform. The effect of Warren Fisher's work was to establish the Treasury as the organizing department for the whole Home Civil Service, as well as the department responsible for national finance. The Treasury still discharges this function. It lays down the gradings, the pay, and the numbers of staff allowed in each Department; and it negotiates with the Civil Service Staff Associations on all questions of pay and conditions which affect the service as a whole. It does this through a system known as Whitleyism, which I shall describe elsewhere.*

The Machinery of Government Report decided the basic principle on which the work done by the state should be distributed between Departments. This was, and is, that Ministries should be concerned with *subjects*—Health, Labour, Trade and so on—which affected the community as a whole, and not with particular groups of people. The principle only took effect gradually. The Admiralty, for instance, until it became part of the Ministry of Defence, was concerned entirely with the running of the Navy. But the basic idea by which each Ministry is concerned with one aspect of a national whole, lies at the heart of the modern Civil

* See page 85.

Service. It is true that each Ministry in practice has its own clientele and accompanying pressure groups, representing the people most deeply concerned in its subject matter; but the fact remains that each functional Ministry applies to the whole population so far as its own function is concerned, and none deals exclusively with one section of the population only. The result is to knit Whitehall much more closely together than would otherwise be the case.

The Ministries of Health and Labour belong to the period of, and immediately after, the First World War. Others have been added—and even subtracted—since. Among those that have come and gone are Ministries of Supply, Materials, and Information. Recent additions are Ministries of Overseas Development, Technology, and Land and Natural Resources. From being a set of separate rooms Whitehall has become, as it were, one large hangar in which compartments can be moved about like screens to divide up the work of Government in whatever way seems best at a particular time.

There are still some signs of the great divide between the old departments, which had grown up very much in their own way over a century or more, and the newer functional Ministries. The older layer consists principally of the Treasury and—until recently—the Admiralty (each of which had made utterly different patterns out of a mediaeval Great Officer put into commission as 'Their Lordships'); the Board of Trade, which is altogether peculiar in its geology; the Post Office; the two Revenue Departments; and the Departments—strictly speaking the only government offices that should be described by that word—headed by a Secretary of State.

But with a few important exceptions which I shall mention in a moment, these differences between the older and the newer offices are purely vestigial and of antiquarian interest only. This is due to the work of Warren Fisher during the twenties and thirties, already referred to. The officials of the Home Office have the same ranks and the same pay, and are subject to the same rules, as those of the Ministry of Technology. The Queen's and Lord Treasurer's Remembrancer, who heads the Scottish Exchequer, may suggest an older world but is in fact a Chief Executive Officer on a par in all respects with the man in charge of a block of work in the Ministry of Pensions at Newcastle. Only the Foreign Office to some extent escaped the Fisher pattern. Warren Fisher was the first person to assume the title 'Head of the Civil Service', in addition to that of Permanent Secretary to the Treasury.

The significant exceptions to the unimportance of historical origins concern the Revenue Departments, the Departments headed by a Secretary of State, and the Treasury itself. Because there was originally only one Secretary of State, ministers who hold this title are still constitutionally interchangeable. They can, and on occasion do, sign for one another. In the sphere of Commonwealth relations and colonies especially, and of home affairs in England and Scotland this still has some importance, since the heads of all these offices are Secretaries of State.

The constitutional position of the Revenue Departments (Inland Revenue and Customs) is more important. They are headed by real, as distinct from purely vestigial, boards, which consist of senior civil servants, and actually meet like boards of directors; and although the members of these Boards have the same conditions of service as the officials in other offices, they are appointed by a special procedure, known as a patent, to 'manage the duties' which Parliament has voted. They have no constitutional responsibility for the form the taxes take; but they are themselves finally and personally responsible for their assessment and collection. One may say that the Chancellor of the Exchequer gets the revenue, but he does not actually collect it. If you wish to dispute the way the Commissioners assess or collect your tax, you must do it in the courts.

The constitutional oddity of the Treasury reflects its authority as the central government department. The old office of Lord High Treasurer was last occupied by a single person more than 250 years ago, before Queen Anne died. Ever since it has been 'in commission'—i.e. divided among several people, of whom the Chancellor of the Exchequer is one. Most of the others are government whips in the House of Commons, whose part in Treasury business consists in authenticating certain formal documents. But the First Lord of the Treasury (as you can read on the brass plate fixed to the door of 10 Downing Street) is now always the Prime Minister. The fact that the Prime Minister is also a Treasury minister has some significance even today. His principal private secretary is usually drawn from the Treasury staff. All Prime Ministers since the beginning of this century have chosen also to be First Lord of the Treasury.*

Which brings me back to the pattern imposed on Whitehall by Warren Fisher. The key to this pattern is very simple and of great importance for an understanding of the Civil Service. Until Fisher's reforms each department had its own arrangements for accounting for the money it received and spent. Most of them had some kind of finance officer, who was in charge of these arrangements. Fisher established the rule that the 'accounting officer'—that is the civil servant responsible for explaining where the money went—should be no other than the chief civil servant of that department, and so the man responsible under the Minister for its organization

* The last not to do so was Lord Salisbury, who combined his premiership (1895–1902) successively with the posts of Foreign Secretary and Lord Privy Seal. He was also the last Prime Minister to sit in the House of Lords.

and efficiency. Thus the 'accounting officer' and the Permanent Secretary are always one and the same person. His duty cannot be delegated. He, and he alone, is responsible both for day to day efficiency and for the soundness of the financial arrangements. Responsibility and authority are married.

The explanation of what happens to the money Parliament votes must be made to Parliament itself. The way this is done is at the bottom of the whole constitutional position of the Civil Service. The accounts of government departments (called, in civil service language 'Appropriation Accounts', because they show how the money 'appropriated' or earmarked by Parliament for particular purposes has been spent on those purposes and no others) are of course published, signed by the Accounting Officer, and laid before Parliament. They are accompanied by a report made by an official called the Comptroller and Auditor General, who has audit staff under his control in every government department. These auditors can send for any official file they think they may need to follow the course of a particular transaction in which they feel full efficiency in the use of public money may not have been achieved. They can ask for supplementary facts and information from the Department. In the end, every year, the reports of the Comptroller and Auditor General contain a budget of criticisms and question-marks about departmental work, on which the Accounting Officer of the department concerned is examined by the Public Accounts Committee. What the Comptroller chooses to say, and how he says it, are entirely matters for him. The government cannot stop him or direct him, any more than they can control a judge. His salary is guaranteed in a special way, and, like a judge, he can only be removed by a vote in both Houses of Parliament.

The Public Accounts Committee is one of the oldest, most

formidable, and most effective, of the standing committees of the House of Commons. Its chairman is always a leading member of the party in opposition (very often one who has served as a Treasury Minister), thus emphasizing the Committee's role as a critic of the government. During the last years of the Conservative administration the chairman of the P.A.C. was Mr Harold Wilson; and it is said that he found the detailed scrutiny of the whole government machine, which this duty involved, an invaluable experience.

The sittings of the P.A.C. take place in one of the bigger committee rooms in the House of Commons. The layout somewhat resembles a court of law, with the members sitting in a semi-circle at one end of the room, and the witness, in splendid isolation, facing the chairman. At one side sits the Comptroller and Auditor General, and at the other representatives of the Treasury, who, as the central finance department, can always be held to answer on the system of financial control. The atmosphere is invariably formal and searching. The Civil Service is here literally brought face to face with Parliament. Not surprisingly, the preparation for the Accounting Officer's appearance before the P.A.C. is an important item in the annual cycle of any department's work.

The report of the P.A.C. is laid before the House of Commons, and its most noteworthy findings will be debated. It will receive, in any case, a good deal of publicity in the press. The department must publish a reply to the report, either undertaking to correct its faults or giving reasons why they cannot accept the P.A.C.'s suggestions or criticisms.

Such was the system for establishing tautness in the Civil Service designed by Warren Fisher. But since his day further important changes have taken place in the general pattern. These are due, fundamentally, to the changed role of government since the acceptance of Keynesian economics after the war of 1939–1945. It is the business of any government today to manage not just those services, such as foreign affairs, justice, and defence, which are traditionally public; but to maintain the general prosperity of the country. This seems obvious to us today, but it was inconceivable not much more than a hundred years ago. During a sterling crisis in 1847, Queen Victoria wrote to her Prime Minister:

> The Queen ... regrets that the state of the Money Market should still be so uncomfortable, but is sure that the Government cannot by any interference do much to mend matters, though it might easily render them still more complicated, and make itself responsible for a crisis, which it has in no way either brought on or been able to avert.*

Today public expenditure (not all of this, of course, is met from taxation raised directly by Parliament) comes to over 40 per cent of the whole national product. The measures the government takes are thus not only bound to affect, but they are also meant to affect, the economic behaviour of everyone. The growing awareness of this new scope of governmental activity led to profound changes in the organization of the Civil Service which began in 1961, and are still evolving. The Warren Fisher Treasury was like the hub of a wheel, each section of which faced a particular spoke—the department with which it dealt. This served the purpose of internal control, and it made sure that no extra money was given without Treasury authority; but it was not helpful to the government in taking the kind of overall economic decisions that were now called for. It was not easy to judge when the total claims on resources were becoming excessive, or to balance the claims of, say, social services against defence, or to

* Queen Victoria to Lord John Russell, 14 October 1847. *The Letters of Queen Victoria* (John Murray).

measure, shall we say, the load placed on the building industry by the accumulated demands of hospitals, schools, roads, housing, and the nationalized industries.

 The result was the Plowden Committee of 1961—a mixed committee of civil servants and non-official experts—and the reorganization of the Treasury, both internally and in relation to the rest of Whitehall. The task of the Treasury was now seen as threefold, though still interconnected: management of the public service as such; financial control; and economic policy. It was not the job of the Treasury, according to the doctrines of Plowdenism, to re-argue policies already arrived at by the various departments, though the Treasury's financial interest should, they considered, be brought in early in the generation of such policies. The Treasury's job, rather, was to co-ordinate overall and to promote a proper system of control over development. In many ways this gave departments greater independence than the Fisher system allowed them; but it has also brought the Treasury more deeply into departmental thinking, and given that thinking a framework—some might say a ceiling—that was not there before. Fifteen years ago direct contact between an ordinary official in a department and the Treasury was rare. It was the job of the Finance Officer of the Department, and no one else, to 'talk to the Treasury' when the department had settled on its policy. Similarly Treasury officials rarely visited departments or sat in on departmental meetings.

Now all this has changed. The old traditions that if the Treasury was present at a meeting it was in the chair, and that the Treasury dealt with departments on the 'one up' principle (i.e. in any dialogue with the Treasury the departmental official was normally one rank above his Treasury opposite), has now gone. The evolution away from the 'hub'

principle has recently been carried a stage further by the creation of the Department of Economic Affairs and the transfer to it of that part of the Treasury which, following on the Plowden Report, was made responsible for national economic policy.

This has been a very brief account of a history and tradition which is still moving through important changes. The tempo may well quicken in coming years as the Civil Service adapts itself to the ever-increasing integration of our highly complex society. It is not part of my business to try to foresee what forms this further evolution may take. What is certain, however, is that the tradition and history one finds in the Civil Service today is not complete. A period of comparative stability between the wars, which lasted long enough to allow people to form an established picture, has come to an end. The story I have just tried to write has many more chapters to be added—chapters which will, perhaps, differ considerably from those which have preceded them.

CHAPTER IV

GENERALIZERS

LIKE ANY OTHER large organization, the Civil Service is divided broadly into specialists and general purpose people. The specialists have professional or occupational labels—lawyers, doctors, architects, inspectors of schools. The generalizers do not. They are the people who are thought of as typically civil servants, because they are nothing else as well. They are the line regiments of the Civil Service.

They are divided into three main groups, or classes, sometimes called 'Treasury Classes' because they are common to the whole Civil Service and their ranks, pay, and conditions are fixed centrally by the Treasury. These classes are known by the rather misty names of 'Administrative', 'Executive', and 'Clerical'.

At one time these classes were comparatively self-contained, and there was little movement between one and another during a career. But that time has now long past. Movement from the Clerical to the Executive Class is a natural progress of promotion. And nearly half the present Administrative Class, from which the highest posts in the Service are filled, started their careers in other classes. In 1963 nineteen out of twenty-nine Permanent Secretaries had entered the Administrative Class directly. The other ten had come from outside it. For Assistant Secretary the figures were even more striking: 312 out of 742 had not been direct entrants to the Administrative Class. Some people move the other way, from the Administrative to the Executive. The patterns are many.

More than one career I know of, started in the Clerical Class, moved on through the Executive to middling rank in the Administrative Class, and then to an even more responsible post in the Executive Class again.

The Classes are not, in fact, superimposed one above the other. They overlap, both in range of pay and weight of responsibility. The most senior members of the Clerical Class have higher salaries than the most junior in the Executive, and may, in fact, be in charge of a larger number of subordinates. As between the Executive and Administrative the overlap is even broader. The Executive covers posts corresponding in salary and responsibility to the whole range of the Administrative except Permanent Secretary and Deputy Secretary. Indeed it is not impossible that the broad division which I shall be describing in this chapter has become so flexible that it will be found to have outlived its usefulness. It is already quite wrong to describe the Administrative Class as consisting wholly of graduates lording it over the rest of the Civil Service who have come in at eighteen or younger without a degree.

With these important qualifications there are three things which distinguish the Classes from one another : the method of entry on first appointment to the Civil Service; the ranks into which the Classes are divided; and the kind of work which each grade is supposed to do. The numbers of established Civil Servants in each class in 1963 were :

	Men	Women	Total
Administrative (home only)	2,277	186	2,463
Executive (including			
Departmental Classes)	59,341	11,663	71,004
Clerical	80,477	70,994	151,471

The Clerical Class is the simplest in structure, since there are only three ranks, one of which (Higher Clerical Officer) is being discontinued. The two main ones are Clerical Assistant and Clerical Officer (C.A. and C.O.). The work done by C.A.s is for the most part the basic clerical duty one finds in almost any office—filing, dealing with straightforward correspondence, despatching, entering up accounts. Much of it is done in biggish groups. It cannot be said that it differs very much from the modest jobs that many thousands do in business. The C.O. on the other hand is beginning to carry responsibility. He may be in charge of a group of C.A.s, or he may be dealing direct with members of the public over the counter of a Post Office or an Employment Exchange. The man who inspects your passport when you go on holiday may be a C.O., and so may the man or girl who finds your book and brings it to you in the British Museum Reading Room. Some C.O.s are promoted from the typing grades to act as personal assistants (secretaries they would be called in business offices) to senior people. A special allowance is paid for this work. The point is that a great deal of C.O. work is not 'clerical' in the usual sense, and the variety is very great.

The theory of the Executive Class is that it is concerned with management and the carrying out of existing policy, not with the formation of new policy. But since new policy depends to a very great extent on experience of what is happening to the old one, and politics is anyway—as Bismarck said—the science of the possible, not a matter of first principles, this is going to be an inadequate definition in the future. What can be said is that the Executive civil servant has a great deal to do with operational matters, and comparatively little with Parliament, advisory committees, and ministerial meetings. Comparatively little, but by no means nothing. The private secretary to the Chief Government Whip (than which few posts could be more parliamentary) is an

Executive civil servant; so is the officer who makes sure in each Department that the answers to Parliamentary Questions are ready at the right time. Much of the experience and lore of the Civil Service is in the hands or minds of executives. The layout of accounts, for instance, the precedents on methods of fraud or smuggling to which a department has been exposed, the outlook and habits of particular communities : all these are likely to be stored up in the Executive Class.

The structure is complex, and there are no fewer than seven ranks of executive : Executive Officer (E.O.), Higher Executive Officer (H.E.O.), Senior Executive Officer (S.E.O.), Chief Executive Officer (C.E.O.), Senior Chief Executive Officer (S.C.E.O.), Principal Executive Officer (P.E.O.), and one rank still higher, which varies in title with the Department concerned. On the whole—though there are always exceptions—those in the rank of C.E.O. and above are committed to a career in the Executive Class.

The E.O. might be called the subaltern of the Civil Service. He is, indeed, the equivalent of a subaltern in the Ministry of Defence. As such he may find himself either a subordinate in a large garrison or in charge of an outpost. In one of the Whitehall ministries he may be digging out facts or working out estimates for a policy paper; dealing with correspondence from the public; authorizing payments in a Finance Division; acting as private secretary to the Permanent Secretary; auditing; or looking after a working party that is going into some aspect of the department's business. In the field, if that is the right word, he may be authorizing the payment of benefits, investigating frauds, looking after the welfare of war pensioners. When he is a more senior E.O. he may well be managing a branch office with a dozen or so staff.

Management is the key word for the Executive Class. As the E.O. advances up the ladder it is probable that he will move into progressively higher managerial responsibility, covering larger numbers of staff and a wider scale of operations. Almost all direct entrant E.O.s can expect to move to the rank next above—Higher Executive Officer. Most local offices of the social service Ministries are headed by civil servants of this grade, which is also that at which all but a small fraction of departmental correspondence is disposed of. Specially trained H.E.O.s form the main body of the Organization and Methods teams which are constantly surveying procedures to see how they can be improved. H.E.O.s also work in support of Principals making a team in the policy or 'staff' business at headquarters. Much of the work done in what are now called 'Secretariat services' in government departments is also done by H.E.O.s. This is the network which directly services Ministers and Parliament. Thus the assistant Private Secretary to a Minister, the Private Secretary to a Parliamentary Secretary, the Parliamentary Clerk—whose job it is to marshal the Department's parliamentary business and make sure its regulations and orders are properly 'laid' before Parliament—will often be an H.E.O.

Senior Executive Officers (S.E.O.s) manage the larger local offices, and at Headquarters will usually be employed in one of three ways : in charge of biggish blocks of procedural work; handling an aspect of finance or establishment; or working alongside Principals on jobs with a substantial policy content. The overlap between Executive and Administrative at this point is particularly noticeable.

With Chief Executive Officer (C.E.O.), which is the next higher rank, the managerial content becomes clearer again. The officer in charge of the whole Youth Employment Service of the London Region of the Ministry of Labour would be a C.E.O.; so would the officer responsible for the day to day staffing questions and accommodation for a major Whitehall

Ministry—a job in some Departments called 'Chief Clerk'. A great deal of the most responsible work on both staff and finance is done by C.E.O.s and the two still higher ranks in the Executive hierarchy. Thus the whole financial business of a major Ministry in one of the thirteen regions into which the country is divided, will be supervised by a C.E.O.

The higher ranks of the Executive run alongside the middle to senior ranks of the Administrative Class, so that the whole pattern looks something like this:

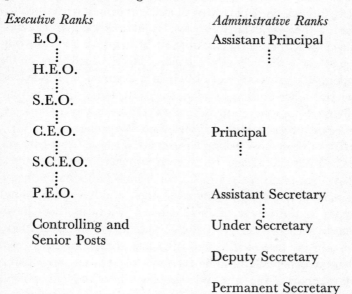

Executive Ranks	*Administrative Ranks*
E.O.	Assistant Principal
H.E.O.	
S.E.O.	
C.E.O.	Principal
S.C.E.O.	
P.E.O.	Assistant Secretary
Controlling and Senior Posts	Under Secretary
	Deputy Secretary
	Permanent Secretary

The dotted lines indicate the existence of salary scales. Where there are no dotted lines the salaries are fixed.

It is often difficult to distinguish, at the lower end of this table, between the managerial and 'policy' content of a given job. Obviously what *can* be done (i.e. the judgment of the manager responsible for the men and machines that will be asked to do it) is an important ingredient in deciding what ought to be done. A simple example, which often occurs in government, is the limitation on what can be printed and distributed in a given time on the enormous scale that is needed for some national operation. But as the machinery of government grows larger and more complex, the importance of the senior managers (S.C.E.O.s, P.E.O.s and above) increases also. These are the men in close contact with computers, large-scale deployment of staff, and major campaigns. Some of them will already have spent a period in straight policy jobs as Principal or Assistant Secretary before moving to what are often called 'Controlling Posts' which may be in London, but are now more often in a regional headquarters or central office outside London, such as those of the Ministry of Pensions at Newcastle, the Post Office Savings Bank at Harrogate, or the Ministry of Health at Worthing.

Most of those now belonging to the Executive Class entered the Civil Service at age 18 or even younger. The older men and women often started in Classes which have passed away long ago—boy clerks, writing assistants—and have seen many changes in the course of their careers. Many of them have taken degrees or other professional qualifications in their spare time, and the best members of the Class are among the wisest and most dependable public servants to be found anywhere. Today, apart from the side-openings into straight policy work that exist at most stages in the Executive ladder, there is a graduate entry as well as an entry at the age of 18. As time goes on, and larger proportions of the abler young people have higher education, one may expect the nature of the entry to Executive Class to change.

I have tried to give a fairly full portrait of the Executive Class because it is the operational part of the service, and is often not given its full weight in descriptive books in comparison with the smaller and more highly selective Administrative Class. If one picture of the Civil Servant is a creature bowed down by 'routine' and 'red tape', another—often, surprisingly enough held by the same person—is a classically educated mandarin with a public school and Oxford or Cambridge background. The latter is the stereotype of the Administrative Class, once known as the 'First Division'.

Heads of departments, their deputies, the immediate civil service advisers to Ministers, and most ministerial private secretaries belong to this class—though, as I have said, it may not have been the class they joined on originally entering the Civil Service. The administrative officials do the work which impinges closest on Parliament. Policy is for Ministers, but the development of policy—both the analysis of questions to be answered before decision, and the ways of carrying out decisions of principle once they have been reached: this is the work of the Administrative civil servant. It is done under considerable pressure. The consequences of a mistaken judgment can be serious and irretrievable. The job can be fascinating, taxing, and frustrating.

There are rather more than 2,500 Administrative Class civil servants, divided into five ranks, the names of which rather overwork the use of the word 'secretary' (as the names of the Executive overwork the word 'officer'). The highest of these, sometimes described simply as 'Secretary', but more properly 'Permanent Secretary' (or in some Departments, Permanent Under-Secretary of State) is the Civil Service head of a large Whitehall department. It is tempting, though to some extent inaccurate, to use a chess analogy here, and describe this officer as the Queen in a set of administrative chessmen in which the Minister is the King—i.e. the conclusive piece whose actual exertions on the administrative board are limited. Then, continuing the metaphor, the next rank below the Secretary (known as 'Deputy Secretary') becomes a castle, with Under-secretaries as bishops and Assistant Secretaries as knights. These are the senior ranks in the class. This 'back row' in a typical Department might consist of a Secretary, two Deputy Secretaries, six or seven Under-secretaries, and perhaps twenty Assistant Secretaries. The Treasury plays the other Departments with a rather larger back row than this, including several Queens.

The front row—pawns my metaphor makes them, but well-placed pawns are powerful pieces—are the Principals and Assistant Principals, the latter being the training grade in which the new entrant from university spends the first few years of service. The Minister's private secretary may be regarded as the King's pawn.

One way of entering the Administrative Class is direct from the university: but about 40 per cent have entered in other ways, and many of these are, in fact, not graduates. Their origins were highly diverse. Thus in 1963 the number of people appointed Principal was 108. Only 37 of these had entered the Service direct from university as Assistant Principals; 22 had transferred from the Executive Class or Departmental Classes by examination or otherwise; 12 had come from other parts of the Civil Service (mainly from the Scientific Civil Service, but there was an auditor and an Air Traffic Control Officer among them); and 37 were appointed direct from outside life.

There are thus two points to be made. The first, mentioned already, is that the opportunities of entering the Administrative Class are far from being confined to 22 year old graduates; secondly, it is not, and will not for many years be, a homogeneous group, like, say, the *Inspecteurs des Finances* in

France. Its members have widely different backgrounds, histories, and educations.

Leaving aside the two highest ranks, the Administrative Class is deployed in two different kinds of way. Most of them work in divisions or branches (the name varies) headed by an Assistant Secretary, and containing two, three, or four Principals. Each such division is concerned with one or another aspect of the department's work. It may be unemployment benefit, or water supplies, or fire services, or finance. The point is that every substantial issue of policy reaching the department within that area of responsibility will come to that division. The solution may conform to a precedent, or it may involve changing a precedent, or it may require a new piece of machinery or a fresh negotiation. Some, such as annual estimates, is determined by the Parliamentary time-table; some, such as working out a piece of legislation, by ministerial pledges *and* the Parliamentary time-table; some may involve working to patterns that have been settled, and some may be working out alternative patterns for choice by ministers.

The other deployment of the Administrative civil servant is in what I have called 'secretariat' posts. Notable among these are the private offices of ministers, which constitute the main bridges between ministers and their departments. The Principal Private Secretary is usually a Principal, but in some departments (e.g. the Treasury) he is an Assistant Secretary, and the private secretary to the Prime Minister is an Under-secretary. For the Cabinet as a whole there is a secretariat headed by an officer of Permanent Secretary rank, which provides the secretaries for all Cabinet Committees as well as the Cabinet itself. In addition the Administrative normally provides the secretariat for Royal Commissions and other government enquiries. In the ordinary way the civil servant

who is detached like this does a two-year spell and then
returns to divisional work, often, though not always, on promotion.

But imaginary examples are very often better than abstract
explanation—though a gift for explanation, either spoken or
written, is perhaps the most valuable of all qualities for an
administrative civil servant. Let us take a look at the ranks,
and possible careers through them taken by two wholly
imaginary, but not untypical, officials.

Henry Halliday and Janet Mason were appointed Assistant
Principals at the same time. Henry had started as an Executive Officer and entered the Administrative Class through the
internal competition limited to serving civil servants, so he,
at 27, was a little older on appointment than Janet. She came
in straight from university with a first-class degree in
economics, at the age of 22.

After a series of courses, including a three-month one at the
Civil Service Centre for Administrative Studies, and two or
three different postings to divisions in their department, learn-
ing on the job and doing some 'live' work, both Henry and
Janet became private secretaries. Henry served a junior
minister, Janet was Assistant Private Secretary, to the Secretary of State. She is now 27, he is 32. Next year they both
'went up' to be Principals. Henry went a bit before Janet;
but let us suppose that in fact Janet has a bit of an intellectual edge on Henry, perhaps more staying power, and a spice
of luck to go with it, at this stage of their lives. She does
some extremely good work as secretary of an interdepartmental committee, and then emerges with credit from an
extremely hot corner, where things could easily have gone
wrong. She is noticed (as is sometimes said) and after only
five years as a Principal she goes back to the private office as

Principal Private Secretary to the Secretary of State. After two years in that exhausting post, making seven years as a Principal all told, she becomes an Assistant Secretary. She is 35. The average age for promotion to that rank is at present about 42.

Janet is now head of a division containing three Principals, and in effective charge of a particular block of work. Henry waits his turn. He has had rather hum-drum postings, and so far has not made much out of them. At this point the department, she is lent to the Treasury for two years, and is the Cabinet Office for two years, and Henry is sent. He does the work outstandingly well—unobtrusively, yet smoothly. He returns, now in his early forties, with an enhanced reputation, and at 42 becomes an Assistant Secretary.

But Janet continues to shine. Having been, in the course of five years, the head of two successive divisions in her Department, she is lent to the Treasury for two years, and is highly successful in a field she has not so far tackled—Overseas Finance. She comes back to her old department just at the moment when a retirement creates a vacancy as Under-Secretary, and although she is by no means the most senior Assistant Secretary, Janet gets it. At 42 she is one of the eight Under-Secretaries in her Department, and is superintending several Assistant Secretary Divisions.

Henry, now 47, is soldiering on, two years, and one rank, junior to Janet, though he remains, alas, as he always was, five years older. He could, it must be admitted, spend another thirteen years and end his career in the same rank. But in this case something equally probable happens. Two years later, just before Henry's fiftieth birthday, the Accountant General—i.e. the chief finance officer—of his Department is permanently transferred to the Treasury. Henry succeeds to the unexpected Under-Secretary vacancy, being by now the senior promotable Assistant Secretary. He proves to be an extremely competent Accountant General. The mixture of experience and grit which had built up over thirty years of Civil Service life make him, in this post, a dominating figure in the department. He is persuasive and benign—qualities he has acquired with age. His advice to ministers on financial questions carry great weight. At the end of only four years he leaves Janet standing and becomes Deputy Secretary in another Department where, at the age of 57 he succeeds the Permanent Secretary as its head.

Sir Henry Halliday retires at 62, after five years in charge of his new Department. Such late and sudden flowerings are by no means uncommon in the Civil Service; nor are careers which fade a little after a brilliant start. Janet might have ended—a not unsuccessful career—as an Under-secretary, even though she would by retirement have spent eighteen years in the rank. But it ends more happily than that. When she is 51 Janet has the opportunity of being elected head of a notable women's college, and leaves the Civil Service on what are called 'approved employment' terms. She still often sees Henry, who is as benign and persuasive as ever.

What had they done in the total of 64 years which between them they had contributed to work in the Administrative Class? During most of it they had had fingers on the pulse of some aspect of national affairs, noting its development at close quarters, knowing what was going to happen next just a little before it was news, thinking round its problems, making and working arrangements within an ever-changing design. As they rose in rank they had seen more and more of the pattern and having passed through the ranks below them they knew, at each stage, how what was decided would affect those who saw less of the pattern than they currently did. They had acquired a very large acquaintance not only inside but outside Whitehall—business people, trade unionists, teachers, professional men—and had made assessments of each. They had handled, and extracted the essence from hundreds of meetings, and written memoranda which, if bound together, would fill a sizeable number of volumes. They had taken work home when the going was hard, and sat up half the night at the House of Commons briefing their minister during midnight debates. At the end of it all their names were relatively unknown, except to some hundreds of people who had faith in their judgment.

CHAPTER V

SPECIALISTS AND SCIENTISTS

THIS IS BOUND to be an untidy chapter. The demand in the public service is for experts of nearly every kind. We are still not at the end of finding out how these experts, who represent so much of what is modern in society, fit best into a civil service which is the servant of ministers responsible to Parliament. What is certain is that no picture of the Civil Service as it is today would be complete without an account of the professionals, and a stress on their growing importance.

The old theory was that the experts were plastered on to the administrative core from outside. They were set specific problems by the administrators, and asked to solve them. The solutions were then sucked back into the administrative machine. Today the professional, be he lawyer, architect, scientist, or engineer, is much closer to the discussions leading up to the technical questions he will be asked to solve. Often a professional will be 'twinned' with an administrator to do a job which would formerly have been either wholly professional or wholly administrative. Examples are the Architects and Buildings Branch of the Department of Education and Science (which is headed jointly by an Architect and an Assistant Secretary), and the Secretariat of the Council for Scientific Policy, whose joint heads are a Scientific and an Administrative Civil Servant.

I shall divide this account into three parts:

(1) Professional advisers—e.g. doctors, lawyers, architects, engineers.
(2) Inspectors
(3) The Scientific Civil Service.

The great difference between all these groups and the generalizers discussed in the last chapter is that within their professional fields their judgments and decision are those of individual professional men. What they say is not just contribution to a general pool of ideas, but specific opinion. In some cases, such as the findings of doctors on pension cases, or actuaries on superannuation funds, their professional opinions are required by legislation, and must be taken publicly into account.

Lawyers are the longest-standing corps of advisers to the Civil Service, and necessarily play a great part in its work. In some countries most civil servants are lawyers themselves; but in England, even if an administrator happens to have a legal qualification, it is no part of his duty to offer advice on legal matters. The civil service lawyer can be involved in many different kinds of legal business. Some are engaged on case work and prosecutions; some in conveyancing and property questions; and some in the preparation of legislation. All government legislation, whether it takes the form of an Act of Parliament, a statutory order, or some other kind of legislation such as an order in council, is written and interpreted by civil service lawyers. They are, in fact, responsible for finding the correct and conclusive language for every decision of the government that is intended to bind the citizen.

The larger government departments have their own legal groups headed by an officer usually known as the Solicitor though he may (like most other legal civil servants) be either a solicitor or a barrister. Below him there will be a number of Assistant Solicitors and Senior Legal Assistants. Departments which have less legal work have it done for them by teams organized under the Treasury Solicitor, who is the Treasury's chief legal adviser. There are also a number of fairly small, but important offices where the entire senior staff are lawyers, because the business is wholly legal in character : the Lord Chancellor's Department; the Law Officers' Department; the Office of the Director of Public Prosecutions; and the Office of Parliamentary Counsel. This last is one of the nodal points in the Civil Service. It is a highly specialized group of barristers who are experts in the drafting of Acts of Parliament. Every measure that the government presents to Parliament has been hammered out by one of these Counsel in consultation with his 'client' Department, who give him his instructions on what the Act is to do. Until the Act is safely on the statute book the hand of its Parliamentary Counsel continues to guide it, making sure that the wording of any amendments Parliament makes are consistent and really do what is required of them.

Doctors are mainly employed by the Health Departments, the Education Departments, and the Ministry of Pensions; but there are also doctors in the Home Office (prisons and forensic medicine); Housing and Local Government (public health); and the Treasury (advising on the medical problems of the Civil Service itself). On the whole the doctor in the Civil Service does not have the care of patients. He is concerned, rather, with what might be called 'medical control' : the assessment of disability, advice on standards, statistics on the incidence of disease, the medical inspection of school children, advice on new drugs. Liaison with the practising medical world is also a vital part of the civil service doctor's job.

The professional status of the expert civil servant has already been mentioned. One of the ways it is emphasized is that on professional matters the man above an expert is always someone who is qualified in his profession. This does not mean that he sees nothing of lay colleagues—or indeed expert colleagues from other professions : but for career purposes lawyers are organized by lawyer superiors, doctors by doctor superiors, and so on. The statisticians in the Civil Service are an interesting illustration. The need for statistical expertise in the Civil Service has been steadily growing, and most big departments now have a statistical group responsible for organizing the quantitative picture of the Department's work. Very often this group will be in charge of a Chief Statistician (approximately Assistant Secretary rank), or even a Director of Statistics, who corresponds to an Under-secretary. At the centre of the government machine, annexed to the Cabinet Office, there is the Central Statistical Office, whose head is also head of the whole government Statistical Service. This interlocking is particularly important, not only because of the nature of statistical work, which must be consistent above all things; but because the statistics produced by one department are very often vital to the planning of other departments. Among the continuing statistical exercises that are essential for a modern economy and are needed by the whole Civil Service, are such measurements as the Cost of Living Index (officially known as the Index of Retail Prices), the Index of Production, the figures for the inward and outward balance of trade, and the Gross National Product at Factor Cost (G.N.P.)—the celebrated 'cake' from which all slices have to come.

The economic advice available to the Government goes back to Keynes, and is now organized in a special 'economist class' spread, like the statisticians, through the departments, but centring, like them, on the Head of the Economic Service in the Treasury. Some departments, notably the Department of Economic Affairs and the Ministry of Overseas Development, have a large staff of economic advisers, some of whom are engaged on research. Among the central tasks of the former group is the preparation and rolling forward of the National Plan; and work with the National Economic Development Council and the 'Little Neddies' for different industries.

A rather different group of professionals is concerned with our physical environment, and centres on the Ministries of Housing and of Public Building and Works. These are the architects, quantity surveyors, planners, and engineers. Unlike the statisticians and economists these groups have no central point of professional reference, but within their own departments they form separate career ladders.

The Government is much the largest employer of engineers in the country : there are nearly 6,000 engineers in all the main branches—civil, electrical, and mechanical. They are supported by some 35,000 technical and drawing office staff. Most of these work in connexion with defence, in the Post Office, and in the Ministry of Public Building and Works. Much of what they do is similar to corresponding professional work elsewhere, and some of it is abroad. But there is also a considerable range of inspectorial and control work— for instance examining plans of an atomic installation from the point of view of safety; inspecting mines and quarries; advising from the point of view of cost on the engineering services proposed for, say, a new hospital.

If the engineering world in the Civil Service is still rather on its own, dealing with specific tasks in an engineering frame of reference, the reverse is true of the architects and the planners. Their skills are brought to bear in the closest possible collaboration with administration. Like the lawyer, the architect and the planner work as members of teams translating policy into a matching product. The development of school building in the last ten years provides an example. Here architects and educational experts, instead of setting one another problems, have sought to pool their skills to design schools which are at the same time efficient for their purpose and economical in construction. Part of a civil service architect's work lies in design of actual buildings, and in development work of a pioneering kind. Another part—more akin to a civil service doctor's—is case-work on plans prepared by other architects working for local authorities, universities, and other public bodies. Here he will be concerned with the standards of building for which public money can be allowed.

The profession of planner is a new one, and intimately bound up with administration. The contemporary world has called it into existence. All over Britain changes in our landscape brought about by new housing, slum clearance, relocation of industry, industrial blight, reafforestation, road and motorway development, extension of water and sewerage schemes, new towns, national parks, are setting problems of integrated planning. It becomes less and less possible to deal piecemeal with the use of land. Plans, co-ordinated into regional studies, involve intricate social, physical, and political questions, and very often a number of government departments, as well as many local authorities.

Two other professions, those of scholar and journalist, must complete* this rapid tour of civil service expertise. The scholars work mainly, though not entirely, in the national museums and galleries, where they are known rather quaintly as 'Keepers'. The journalists are officially styled Information

---

* I have not tried to deal here with many other groups: actuaries, quantity surveyors, dentists.

Officers, and work in the Central Office of Information and in the Information Divisions of departments.

Most of the public museums, libraries and galleries are now grouped under the Education Departments, and in some ways could be said to form a world quite separate from administration. The Keeper of Greek and Roman Antiquities at the British Museum has as many affinities with the universities as with the Department of Education and Science. But the points of administrative contact are there nevertheless. A new building project brings in the architects and financial administrators alongside the librarians and curators, besides arousing public interest on a scale that is quite likely to bring Parliamentary Questions or a debate in the House of Lords. The need to 'save' some national treasure, such as the Goya (or to recover it); the policy on the export of works of art; the tourist attractions of our national collections; all these can bring in the Board of Trade or the Treasury, the Home Office and the Board of Customs and Excise. Then there is the Public Record Office, the home not only of Magna Carta and historical records reaching even further back than that, but the ultimate repository of all the paper produced by the Civil Service that is worth keeping. The question of what *is* worth keeping is a big one in itself, given that it costs money to keep things. There are carefully framed rules about the life and ultimate disposal of all official files. It might be thought that here, at any rate, is a quiet corner. But the hand of politics, and so of Parliament, can ruffle even the archives, as the story of the Casement Diaries shows. Strong pressure was brought to bear on the Government recently to allow these diaries of the Irish nationalist hero of the 1914–18 war to be put on the open shelves.

Even the archives are not the ultimate in civil service scholarship. In the Cabinet Office there is a small section of professional historians, with the duty of gradually distilling official history from the vast accumulation of the government's records.

The Information Officers, on the other hand, are concerned with the breath of today, and with what a department has to tell the public through press, radio, and television. Of all the groups in the Civil Service, the Information Officers have to be most careful about the boundary between carrying out the policy of ministers and making party propaganda. The Information Officer's job is basically to keep in touch with the various publicity media (particularly the 'trade' and professional press concerned with his department) on the one hand; and with the various branches of his department for everything that needs publicity. Often a department will want to run a campaign—on some aspect of road safety for instance, or on some change in social service legislation which involves a great many people in doing something to obtain its benefit. Such campaigns will be worked out by the administrators with the Information Officer, perhaps bringing in the Central Office of Information and the Stationery Office as well.

Campaigns like this often mean translating ideas from one kind of language into another. One of the most interesting things about Civil Service life is to see the different ways in which something is expressed for different purposes. Proposals will start, perhaps, conversationally, round a conference table, and perhaps at that point there will be a few slang phrases coined to express key ideas. Then the whole thing gets worked out in detail—let us assume these are proposals for legislation —in clear but pedestrian civil service language. Then the parliamentary lawyer will cast it into the specialized and highly allusive language of the statute book. His job is not unlike writing a computer programme, and the product is

often about as intelligible to ordinary people as binary nota-
tion. The point is that it leaves no room for doubt. Next the
minister in charge of the Bill explains it in a series of speeches,
step by step, to Parliament. Finally the new Act must be cast
into leaflets and advertisements by the Information Services.

An Inspectorate, in the Civil Service, is a countrywide
organization of officers, enforcing standards laid down in legislation. Inspectors normally work as individuals, not as members of teams, and although they have their own hierarchy
within the department to which they belong, each has a great
deal of discretion in his or her own area. So they are a rather
special kind of civil servant, and since they often need a
specialist qualification, I have included them in this chapter.
Very often an Inspectorate is the main link between central
and local government for a particular service. There are
many Inspectorates, but the main ones are the Inspectors of
Taxes, the Inspectors of Schools, and the Inspectors of Factories.*

The Inspector of Taxes is the person who decides how
much tax the law requires a particular individual to pay. It is
his duty to judge whether deductions claimed for expenses are
justified, what allowances should be made for trading losses,
and what assessment should ultimately be made. He must, of
course, do his best to be consistent, and in this he will get some
guidance from senior inspectors. But the decisions are his, and
can be challenged in the courts. His work needs a rather
uncommon combination of skills, which are perhaps closer to
those of the accountant, than to any other profession. He
must have a knowledge of the law, both on taxation, and on

* Others are Mines Inspectors; Planning Inspectors (who enquire
into objections to town planning proposals); Inspectors of Railways;
Inspectors of Constabulary.

business generally; must have insight into accounts; be a patient and firm negotiator; and possess even more discretion than most civil servants.

Some inspectors of taxes have entered the Inspectorate from other classes of the Civil Service, mainly the Executive. Others—about sixty a year—come in through the same competition as the Administrative Class. And a surprisingly large number of senior civil servants have at one time been inspectors of taxes.

The job of the Inspector of Factories is to make sure the law on working conditions is being observed, and to raise standards of safety. He is often a qualified engineer, and may specialize in some particular aspect of industry. Some are doctors. Altogether there are about 500 Factory Inspectors, distributed throughout the country. A good deal of their time is spent in visiting factories, docks, construction sites. Sometimes these visits are by arrangement, sometimes unannounced. But he is not mainly, or even chiefly, trying to catch firms out in breaking the law. He offers expert advice about health and safety. As industrial life grows more and more complex, the hazards become more complex and technical too. A new chemical process, for instance, can lead to disease if precautions are not worked out and taken—and this can bring the Factory Inspector into contact with the Medical Research Council. New building techniques need to be looked at for new risks, and an Inspector may find himself discussing these with experts from the Ministry of Public Building and Works.

Maintaining standards—this time in education—is also the duty of the Inspectors of Schools, who form a distinct arm of the two Education Departments. Here again the work is a great deal more than visiting schools to make sure that all is in order. The Inspector is a bridge for ideas. Commonly he has himself been a teacher. His ideas, and the ideas he collects from his colleagues in the Inspectorate can go a long way in shaping the schools and further education colleges on his circuit; and his experience of the schools and colleges is fed back to the local education authorities, and to the policy makers, the building programmers, the architects, and the committee secretaries at headquarters. On the whole, because they must have had from five to fifteen years' teaching experience, Inspectors of Schools come later in life to the Civil Service than most other groups. This gives them a particular professionalism. They straddle the worlds of administration and teaching, and work equally closely with both.

Not many people understand that in the Scientific Civil Service alone—a part of the Civil Service I have not even mentioned yet—the government employs more university graduates than it does in the Administrative Class. The establishments in which the Scientific Civil Service mainly works are all over the country, from Torry, near Aberdeen, where research is carried on into fisheries and oceanography, to the Regional Pest Office of the Ministry of Agriculture at Cardiff and the Admiralty Experimental Diving Station at Portsmouth. An immense range of work is covered—forensic science, weaponry, locust control, radar, the weather. Some is basic research, some comes very near to manufacturing things. But on the whole this is a world of applied science, working on specific practical problems.

The research stations vary in their size, in their jobs, and in the Ministries they come under. A good many are affiliated to the Ministries of Defence or Aviation; but the Ministries of Technology, Agriculture, Public Building and Works, Power, and Overseas Development, as well as the Home Office and the Post Office, all have one or more. The scientific department of the National Gallery, the Assay Office of the Mint, and the research laboratories of museums, are all staffed by Scientific Civil Servants. And so is the Patent Office of the Board of Trade, where applications for patents are examined by scientifically expert civil servants.

Each of the government's research stations works as an independent unit, and many of the staff, especially those in what are called the Experimental Officer and Scientific Assistant classes, are taken on locally, and therefore temporarily, in the first place. Those who are taken on like this can compete later through central competitions to become permanent.

Altogether there are about 15,000 scientific civil servants, of whom about 3,500 are in the Scientific Officer class, and the rest in the other two. Scientific Officers are almost all graduates with first or second class degrees. To be an Experimental Officer one needs five G.C.E. passes, of which two must be science A-levels, a pass degree, or a Higher National Certificate. The qualification for Scientific Assistant is four G.C.E. passes, of which one must be in maths and another in English. Movement from any of these classes to another (as well as from rank to rank within them) is possible, provided one has the higher educational qualification; thus such movement is rarer than between say, the Executive and the Administrative on the other side of the Civil Service.

A slang word is always coined for anything new, and the ordinary English for a Scientific Officer is 'boffin'—which came in just about the time the Scientific Civil Service was invented. Since boffins are needed for particular jobs rather than for general service, a great deal of the recruitment is by advertisements for actual vacancies, followed by interview. In the ordinary way people with only first degrees can enter for these jobs up to the age of 29; for those with post-graduate degrees as well the age limits are a bit higher. A great many of the boffins, therefore, have had jobs in universities or industry before coming to work—very often in a similar field —for the government.

The links between the research establishments, the universities, and industry are growing closer all the time. Some people are doing advanced degrees while working at government Research Establishments. Much of the work done has an industrial slant. So far as its scientific work is concerned each establishment works as a unit, not as part of an administrative hierarchy. The Experimental Officers, who would be called technicians and senior technicians in most laboratories outside the Civil Service, and the Scientific Assistants who do the simpler measuring and ancillary jobs, may well pass a whole career in one establishment. Unless the work is secret or special in some way there is little to distinguish them as civil servants except their ranks, their leave, and their pension arrangements, which are very like those I have described elsewhere for the corresponding generalizers.

But as science enters more and more into government and society, administration becomes more and more important in science. This has led to two developments for the more senior scientific civil servant. The establishments I have been describing are run by scientists, so that the government scientist who is promoted in his own establishment becomes concerned with management. Like his administrative colleagues he begins to deal in staffing questions, buildings, money, and planning for the future. Above the rank of Principal Scientific Officer (salary of up to about £3,000 a year) there is an increasing administrative tinge in the work. Pure boffinry ends at Principal Scientific Officer.

The second is that the administrative sides of Whitehall departments are discovering they have managerial jobs for which a man who has worked as a professional scientist is particularly suitable. Often these jobs are in double harness with an administrator of the generalizing kind—the joint secretaryship, for instance, of a scientific committee. In coming years a good many men and women who go into the Scientific Civil Service will probably go into jobs like this. It is all part of the tendency to move away from employing experts in separate groups, and into a kind of 'mixed manning'.

In the lower grades of the Scientific Civil Service there may also be changes making them a more varied career than they are today. At present the two senior ranks of technician both overlap in salary with the Principal Scientific Officer; but in the rank immediately below them there is a great variety of work, some of which has more, and some less serious scientific content.

From this very compressed catalogue of civil service experts I have tried to make only two general points. The first is that the professional judgment of the expert civil servant, whether he is an Inspector of Schools, a lawyer, an actuary, or a scientist, is his own. One of the reasons for having professional people in the Civil Service is so that they can advise on their profession's outlook, as well as give professional judgments; and they could not do the one, unless they could exercise the other. The second point is that although there are still many professional 'pockets' in the Civil Service, where one profession or another dominates, the general tendency is away from this kind of consultant status—the feeling that an expert is called in when matters have got too difficult for the run of the mill civil servants. The expert is now put at the elbow of the administrator (and the other way round) as part of the decision-making process.

CHAPTER VI

RECRUITMENT AND CONDITIONS
OF SERVICE

THIS CHAPTER IS mostly concerned with outlines of facts and rules about how to enter the various parts of the Civil Service, the conditions on which one agrees to serve, and the regulations for retirement and pension. But there is one general point to be made at the beginning of it.

I describe elsewhere the history and principles which have led to the present rules. Some people argue that the emphasis on open competition and complete impartiality which dominates the Civil Service examination and promotion systems is no longer needed to prevent corrupt or inefficient civil servants from being appointed or advanced. This may be so. We may indeed be, as a nation, more competent and more honest than the Victorians as well as better off. But even if this is so, it is not the whole story. As the Select Committee on Civil Service Recruitment say in their recent report,* 'the requirement of public competition was introduced at a time when it was judged essential to demonstrate that political favouritism and private patronage were no longer being employed to introduce incompetent men into the Civil Service'. Even if people introduced into the Civil Service by political favouritism or private patronage were entirely competent, the result would still be unsatisfactory and undemocratic. The present system is directed as much against patronage as it is in

* Sixth Report of the Estimates Committee, Session 1964–65—Recruitment to the Civil Service, para 96.

favour of suitability. The undergraduate with a picturesque or 'non-conforming' record and the rather conventional Assistant Secretary in Laburnum Avenue can both depend on impartial assessment of their merits—one in the entrance exam, the other for promotion. There is no need, in the Civil Service as it is, to curry favour or demonstrate adherence to one set of political opinions rather than another. Advice must be given within the terms of reference of policy: but it need not be trimmed in such a fashion that its acceptability can be foretold in advance. It is very often from the differences of opinion among their official advisers about the right analysis of the facts, that ministers can best make the judgments that then become the frameworks of policy.

All civil servants are either 'established' or 'temporary'. 'Established' means in effect that a permanent career is offered, subject to efficiency, up to the age of 60, at which age the civil servant has the right to take his pension and his Department has the right to ask him to do so. But subject to these rights on either side he may go on after 60 in established service from year to year, or he may continue on a temporary basis. The average age of actual retirement is rather above 60. The temporary civil servant is one who is not guaranteed a permanent career, but he may, and often does, become established in the course of his service, in which case there are arrangements for counting his temporary service towards pension.

I shall deal in what follows mainly with the recruitment of established civil servants, all of which is done through the Civil Service Commission. The Commission are wholly independent in carrying out their job of assessing the qualities and qualifications of candidates. The underlying principle on which they work is to examine 'the general ability and capacity to learn rather than knowledge of the work the future civil servant will be required to perform'.* This, of course, applies to the main classes, not to the specialists.

Apart from personal qualities tested by interview, examination, educational record, and statements given by a candidate's own referees, the Commissioners have to be satisfied that the intending permanent civil servant has reasonably good health and is a British subject or a citizen of the Irish Republic.† For health a medical examination may be required —the standard is probably much the same as that of a 'good life' for life insurance purposes. Both men and women are eligible for all the competitions, but there are one or two classes to which only men are appointed (e.g. Assistant Postal Controller). A woman can be appointed to the Home Civil Service whether she is married or not.

Entry to the Clerical Class is open from 16 upwards on the basis of O-level results and an interview. The upper age limits for the competition vary, being sometimes as high as 60, since here, as elsewhere, the Civil Service faces increasing competition from other employers.‡

The Executive Class competition now also casts its net very wide indeed. Anyone between the ages of $17\frac{1}{2}$ and 23 who has either (a) a university degree; or (b) five G.C.E. passes of which one is in English Language and two are at A-level

---

* The British Civil Service: C.O.I. Pamphlet R 5599, 1963, p. 13.

† For the Home Civil Service, note the broader condition 'British Subject', rather than the stricter 'Citizen of the United Kingdom and Colonies', which, broadly, is required for the Diplomatic Service. The rules are more complicated than this, and there are some possibilities for exceptional cases. If in doubt the Civil Service Commissioners should be consulted.

‡ For details of the rules about eligibility and the exams themselves the official publications of the Civil Service Commission, 21 Savile Row, London W.1 should be consulted.

obtained at the same examination, can enter the competitions. There are interviews (there is no written exam) held in various parts of the country three times a year—in January and May for candidates between $17\frac{1}{2}$ and 23, and in September for those between $17\frac{1}{2}$ and $19\frac{1}{2}$ only.

For direct entry into the Administrative Class (as distinct from transfer into it from one of the other classes in the course of one's career) and for what are known as the Special Departmental Classes (notably the Tax Inspectorate) a university degree is virtually essential. Strictly speaking one of the two methods of entry—by written examination—does not require a degree, but since the exam is itself of honours degree standard the effect is much the same. It is safe to say that so far as the Administrative Class is concerned a candidate with less than a good second class degree has little chance of success by either of the methods of entry; but a good second as compared with a first is not a serious drawback, and the degree can be in pretty well any subject. In the five years 1957 to 1963 the results looked like this :

Candidates with degrees in :	Competed	Successful
History	962	151
Social Studies	632	80
(including Law and Oxford P.P.E.)		
Modern Languages	586	37
Classics	530	111
English	218	23
Science and Maths	98	15
Others	564	46

Of the successful candidates only 39, or less than 10 per cent had less than an upper or undivided second class degree.

Although the traditional arts subjects still predominate, and science candidates are few (perhaps because science opens up other possibilities, including the Scientific Civil Service) the proportion of scientists who succeeded was as high as among those who had studied history. Modern languages and English Literature show the weakest proportion of success. Only about a third of the successful candidates came from boarding schools; but 90 per cent had been at Oxford or Cambridge. These universities have a long tradition of aligning their students towards the Civil Service exams, and at the time in question were still providing something like 20 per cent of all university places in this country.

There are two kinds of examination, known officially as Method I and Method II, and candidates can choose between them or take both : but a certain proportion of candidates is always appointed from those who compete under Method II. Broadly Method I is a full written exam of university honours standard, and Method II a series of personal tests, sometimes known as 'the country house'.

For Method I there is a qualifying written test (Essay, English, and General papers), in April; an interview for those who qualify, followed by a written examination at honours degree standard in subjects chosen by the candidate. Up to 900 marks can be earned on the written examination, and up to 300 on the interview.

The candidates under Method II take the same qualifying examination, and those who pass spend two days living together in groups of five or six, and taking a series of personal and intellectual tests conducted by serving civil servants, psychologists, and other experienced persons. The original pattern for this method was the personnel selection board evolved during the war for picking army officers, but the tests themselves have changed, and their emphasis has, of course, shifted. Finally the candidates under Method II come before the same Interview Board procedure as those who have sat Method I.

For all specialized posts in the Civil Service, and for the Scientific Civil Service, selection is by competitive interview. The vacancies, and the requirements on age, standard of qualification and so forth, are advertised from time to time, but the various qualifying conditions are usefully tabulated in *Civil Service Posts for Graduates* and *The Scientific Civil Service* both published by the Civil Service Commission.

When the civil servant is appointed he or she is assigned to a department. Very often this will be the department the candidate has chosen (one is asked for one's preference), but the decision is made by the Commission, and whether one gets one's choice or not depends to some extent on the distribution of vacancies in that particular year, how many other people have chosen it, and what marks one got in the exam.

For the general classes, training is given during the preliminary years of service, and a great deal of time and attention is now given to this. Clerical and Executive entrants are trained within their own Departments—this may involve attending residential training centres for courses, and day release for courses in Further Education. The administrative class entrant, apart from any other training within the department, will attend the three-month course given at the Centre for Administrative Studies, with its highly concentrated curriculum in economics, administration, and governmental method.

Conditions of service are more or less the same for all varieties of civil servant. Most of them work a five-day week of between 42 and 46 hours; but when there is more work to be done than can be got into those hours it has to be done just the same. Overtime rates are payable to ranks up to and including Executive Officer.

The minimum leave allowance is 15 working days (i.e. three weeks) a year on first entering, and this works up to a maximum of 30 days (i.e. six weeks). Apart from this there are public holidays, including the Queen's official birthday, total-ling $8\frac{1}{2}$ days a year. The annual leave allowance can be spread through the year (which usually runs, for this purpose from November to November) as one wishes, but arrangements are naturally made in each branch or section to make sure that the office is adequately staffed all the year round. This is usually done by circulating a list early in the year on which each member of a branch can enter proposals. When everyone has made their suggestions there may be adjustments, but it is very much a tradition that anyone wanting a particular period on the calendar for a good reason should have it if at all possible.

The arrangements for sick-leave and maternity leave are still generous by standards elsewhere. Sick leave of up to three days is allowed without a medical certificate; and sick leave on full pay is given for up to six months in any period of twelve—of course subject to a doctor's certificate. After that, if illness continues, up to a further six months is allowed on half pay. If a civil servant has to retire through ill-health and has served ten years or more, he receives a proportionate pension. Established women civil servants are entitled to maternity leave as part of normal sick leave for two months, or more if medically necessary. In consideration of this a civil servant either does not claim any national insurance benefit to which he may be entitled while still serving, or the pay he receives while on sick leave is reduced by that amount.

In principle a civil servant is required to serve where he is sent, and he may be transferred from one department or one part of the country, to another. There is at present a major programme for moving civil service work out of London wherever possible. A civil servant may also ask to be moved, and in departments with a major regional network vacancies are often advertised by internal circular, so that people with personal reasons for moving can put in for them. When a civil servant has to move in the interests of the service his expenses—including the cost of re-establishing himself in a new home, are paid.

For the civil servant with personal problems or difficulties there is someone to turn to in the Welfare Officer of each Department. There are many ways in which he—or more often she—can help. Most departments have staff benevolent funds from which grants or loans can be made to people hit by sudden misfortunes. There is a Civil Service Santorium Society with a modest subscription, to which many civil servants belong : it covers the expenses of cancer and tuberculosis for a civil servant and his dependents. Queen Victoria's favourite country residence, Osborne, in the Isle of Wight, is now a convalescent home to which civil servants as well as naval, military, and Air Force officers can go to recover from illness. Mass radiography and the collection of blood for blood banks are often to be found going on in government offices.

The general conditions under which civil servants work, and any grievances and representations they may want to make about them, are dealt with by a system of joint consultation between the government as employer and the various staff associations. A civil servant may belong to any association that covers his job (but he does not *have* to belong to any), among the principal associations being :

The Civil Service Clerical Association (C.S.C.A.)

The Union of Post Office Workers (U.P.O.W.)

The Society of Civil Servants (S.C.S.)

The Civil Service Union (C.S.U.)

The Institution of Professional Civil Servants (I.P.C.S.)

The Federation of Civil Service Professional and Technical Staffs (F.C.S.P.T.S.)

The Association of First Division Civil Servants (F.D.A.)

The Inland Revenue Staff Federation (I.R.S.F.)

The names of these are for the most part self-explanatory. The C.S.C.A. is the association of the Clerical Class, the S.C.S. of the Executive class, the F.D.A. of the Administrative class, and the C.S.U. of such grades as messengers, liftmen, and paper-keepers.

Representatives of these and other staff associations form what is known as the 'staff side' of National and Departmental Councils called Whitley Councils; the other 'sides' of which are made up of civil servants concerned with staff management questions at the national or departmental levels whichever the case may be. These councils provide a great deal more than a means of discussing grievances and difficulties. They enable departments to sound the staff's own opinion about the most convenient ways of carrying out decisions which affect the work the staff will be doing. Any big change in procedure will usually have been discussed with the staff side first, and there is a great deal of informal, as well as formal contact on this sort of subject. The Staff Side secretary is a key man for the general happiness and efficiency of the office, and a week will rarely pass in a busy department when he does not have some contact with the establishment officer who acts as secretary of the Official Side.

One subject which concerns staff associations and Whitley Councils a great deal is the procedure for reporting on staff and for promotion. This varies from department to department in detail; but annual reports are made by senior colleagues on very nearly every civil servant, and these naturally are important when he is being considered for promotion. If a report is exceptionally unfavourable it is the normal rule that the civil servant concerned should be shown it. In some departments reports are submitted up the line so that two or three levels above the reporting officer can say what they think, which will often aim at evening out any variation in standards between different reporting officers. In others all reports are referred to an independent group of officers who try to get a common standard. The point is to work a system in which reports are as fair and objective as possible, and to eliminate favouritism, over-severity, soft-heartedness, and prejudice.

In reports a man is always measured both in the job he is doing and the job above it; and it is one of the maxims of the Civil Service that ability to do the first adequately—or even well—is no proof of how one will perform in the second. Nor does seniority in itself give any right to promotion, though it gives the right to be considered when promotions are being made. A man may be passed over twice, or even three times in favour of a junior, but his claims will still be fairly considered again next time. Promotions—except to the very highest ranks—are made by departments, so that the opportunities vary at different times and in different parts of the service, since promotions are only made to fill actual vacancies. But at some levels there are arrangements for pooling promotions over the whole service so as to even out prospects for those who are prepared to change their department on promotion.

Over most of the Civil Service, promotion is done by boards of senior officers who interview those who are 'in the field' (i.e. have a certain agreed seniority), and make recommendations to the head of the department. In some departments it is possible to appeal against non-promotion to a second board. Permanent Secretaries are appointed by the minister in charge of the department in consultation with the Treasury; and they, together with certain other key appointments, such as Principal Finance Officer and Principal Establishment Officer, must be approved by the Prime Minister.

At what sort of age can promotion be expected on average? Averages can be dangerously misleading, and because of the varying age structures of departments and the development or contraction of government business at different periods, luck can play its part. A man who is promoted at a time when government activity is increasing might have had to wait longer, or perhaps never have been promoted at all during a quieter period. Sometimes a man will stay for many years in one rank and then pass through two or three higher ones in quite a short time, as happened to a Permanent Secretary of the Treasury who sat, I believe, for eighteen years as a Principal. But looking at matters broadly as they are, an entrant to the Administrative Class could look forward to being a Principal shortly before thirty, and to promotion as Assistant Secretary at just over forty. In the Executive Class the move from Executive Officer to Higher Executive Officer is likely to come in the thirties and to Senior Executive Officer in the forties. But there are innumerable exceptions. I know a man who started as an Executive Officer and, after moving into the Administrative class as a Principal became an Assistant Secretary at 44; a woman entrant as an Assistant Principal who became an Assistant Secretary well before 40 and an Under Secretary at 42; and, conversely, men who have retired as Principals.

What about rewards, in the strictly financial sense? A civil servant's income (apart from any private means he may have —and few do) is his pay. He has no fringe benefits, such as the use of a car or business expenses apart from travelling expenses if he travels on duty. The pay for each grade, except the highest of all is fixed on what is known as the principle of 'fair comparisons': that is to say 'comparison with the current remuneration of outside staffs employed on broadly comparable work, taking account of differences in other conditions of service.' This job of comparative fact-finding is done by a special independent unit known as the Pay Research Unit. For the highest posts (down to Assistant Secretary and the equivalent) there is a special Review Body.

Any attempt to describe the exact pay structure of the Civil Service would be far too lengthy for this book, and would in any case run the risk of being obsolete very quickly. Adjustments, major and minor, are constantly made. Things are further complicated by the fact that most civil servants are paid on incremental scales by which their pay increases each year up to a maximum; and rates are slightly higher in London than elsewhere. Only the most general indications therefore are possible. The responsibilities carried by the head of a major Government Department are salaried at about £8,500 a year. The more senior posts below this from Assistant Secretary and the equivalent upwards cover the range from between £3,500 and £4,500 to about £6,500. The middling posts (Principal, Chief and Senior Executive Officers, Principal Scientific Officer etc.) come in the bracket from just under £2,000 to rather over £3,000. The new entrant to the Administrative or Executive Classes or the Scientific Civil Service will be paid upwards of £800 a year to begin with.

Rank for rank salaries are the same throughout the service; men and women are paid the same; and all salaries are public knowledge. The fact that with very little trouble one can work out exactly what pay a given civil servant must be getting removes an important ground for jealousy and suspicion. There are no private deals, no hidden payments.

Finally comes pension. The civil servant does not pay any contributions towards his pension, but he must now do so (if he is a man) towards a pension for his widow if he dies in service. Leaving the widow's pension aside a civil servant is entitled, when he retires, to a pension equal to one eightieth of his average salary over the last three years for each year up to a maximum of 45 that he has served. In addition he receives a lump sum of three years' pension. Thus a civil servant who retired after 40 years established service, and had received pay of £2,400, £2,450 and £2,500 in each of the last three years, would get a pension of forty eightieths of £2,450—i.e. £1,225, plus a lump sum of £3,675. The pension is reduced by 26 shillings a week in respect of National Insurance, and since no graduated contributions are paid by or for civil servants into the National Insurance scheme, there is no graduated National Insurance pension. The balance of National Insurance pension, above 26 shillings a week, is payable in addition to civil service pension.

Not all civil servants, of course, serve so long as in my example, and the pension scheme takes account of this. In general there is a minimum of ten years' service for pension rights, but temporary civil servants with at least five years are entitled to a lump sum, and a woman who resigns on marriage after six years' service or more receives a payment of a month's salary for each year's service. Thus a woman who served from 20 to 26 and was then getting £1,200 a year, would receive a dowry of £600. Several important rules cover those who decide not to make the Civil Service a life career. For a large range of jobs outside the Civil Service (e.g. teaching, local government) the civil service pension earned by service so far can be as it were 'frozen', and is payable on ultimate retirement. The same is true for a civil servant who leaves when he is 50 or over. When he is 60 he can take the pension earned by his service.

In general the Civil Service has always in the present century claimed to be a 'good employer' : and so it is, within the limitations imposed by the fact that in a public service public policy must come first. One aspect of public policy is of course a contented, fairly treated, and therefore efficient Civil Service.

CHAPTER VII

RED TAPE: A CIVIL SERVANT'S WORK

THE PHRASE 'RED TAPE' comes almost automatically to mind when the Civil Service is mentioned. It is even the title of one of the leading Civil Service professional journals. The words are indefinite yet powerful, like so many that take root in the mind. The 'tape' part suggests entanglement and restriction of an unnecessary, even childish kind (we meet tape more often in childhood than when we are grown up). If one is really determined to restrict, one uses iron, or brass, not tape, so there is also a suggestion that given good-will, efficiency and energy, a 'tape' restriction can be cut through.

The 'red' part is also important. It brings in the idea of fussiness and obsolescence. Nobody nowadays, except a lawyer, actually uses red tape for tying up official papers, and most people know this. Which makes the image of people using out-of-date methods to frustrate sensible objectives all the more potent.

The general effect of the phrase is a feeling that the civil servant's work, so far as it consists of 'red tape', is lacking in intellectual quality. The civil servant, according to this picture, knows about and manipulates *procedure*, whether it makes sense in a given situation or not. If the right form has not been filled in, if the correct rubber stamp has not been applied, an obstruction results, and 'red tape' is in action. An important part of this picture is that the official does not look beyond the actual defect of procedure, or consider whether there is any sense in the situation. People very often feel like this when they have been prevented by an official agency from doing something they want to do.

It is undoubtedly true that where there are rules—and servants are concerned with rules—there will be restrictions, and these may well be unimaginative or apparently unimaginative. There are two main reasons for this, apart from the general fact that nobody likes having his personal wishes frustrated. First, the desire of public authorities, from Parliament downwards, is to be satisfied that their wishes have been carried out; and secondly, the fact that the complexity of society always tends to outrun the adequacy of administrative arrangements, however carefully these are devised. In a perfect society there would be no complaints about red tape because the arrangements would have taken account of every case that could rationally occur, and every argument that could rationally be made. The only people who were restricted would immediately understand why, and would therefore never complain. It is the aim of the civil servant in his work to produce arrangements that will approximate as nearly as possible to this ideal.

Such work is often thought of, just the same, as uncreative, as having no apparent product. The civil servant does not—on this view—make discoveries like the scientist, produce solutions to physical problems, like the engineer, cure, teach, or give pleasure, like the doctor, the schoolmaster, or the actor. Even if one allows that many scientists never make discoveries or that some actors fail to give pleasure, the essential comparison between the creative and the uncreative remains. But it is false.

Discoveries in administration are probably as important for society as discoveries in science. They are less noticeable, because the most successful administrative discoveries quickly become part of our everyday habits. They must do so, otherwise they would not be successful administrative discoveries. It is almost impossible to believe that they were actually made by some man sitting at his desk sucking his pen, and then developed—perhaps against ingrained administrative habits—much as Columbus developed his idea that the earth was a sphere. Many such discoveries, like many scientific discoveries, are technical, and are therefore difficult to describe. But I will give four examples to show what I mean.

The Bonded Warehouse. This was invented by English administrators early in the eighteenth century, and without it the development of international trade would have been seriously hampered. Until the bonded warehouse was invented, goods on which customs duty was payable could not be unloaded from the ship in which they had arrived until the duty was paid. But to pay the duty on a whole ship-load of brandy before some at least had been sold, meant that importers had to have large sums of unemployed money on hand. The ship could not wait indefinitely, unloading its cargo bit by bit. Things were still worse if the idea was to re-export some of the cargo in another ship, making a market profit. The duty had to be paid, and then reclaimed when the goods were exported. This was real red tape.

The solution to this was to say that goods could be unloaded at once from ships into special warehouses without paying any duty; and that the duty would be collected as and when the goods left the warehouse for sale. If the goods only left the warehouse for re-export, no duty would be collected at all. The thing seems extraordinarily simple; but the effects were far reaching.

Prepaid Postage by Stamp, was one of the most decisive

administrative inventions ever made, equalling in importance the discovery of steam power. It is not, intellectually speaking, a simple idea, for it involves three separate administrative concepts: uniform rates regardless of actual distance; payment in advance; and a form of evidence for the payment (an adhesive stamp) which is portable until it is used, and can then easily be deprived of validity (by being cancelled) while still remaining as evidence of payment.

Points Rationing is a more recent example, and a solution to what seemed an insoluble problem of wartime rationing. The more common foods, such as butter, bacon, meat and cheese, could be dealt with by allowing each person so many ounces a week and giving him a book containing dated coupons for each food, which the shopman could cut out when he sold the allowed amount. But what should one do about the vast variety of tins, which even in wartime were very different in size and nutritional value? They had to be rationed, but when tinned chicken, say, came in 2lb tins, did one make a rule that enough meat coupons (at 8oz a week per person per week) had to be given up? And how did one put that over? And what about tinned fruit and tinned vegetables? Did one have a special ration for tins, and if so how did one measure the value of each tin?

The answer was to put an extra set of coupons in each ration book with numbers on them showing the 'points' each represented for a month; and then to 'price' each kind of tin in terms of those points. People were allowed to save up their points to get one of the more valuable tins, but of course the total amount each could get was rationed by the number of points in each book, which was the same for everybody. The ministry could change the 'points' value of different tins depending on the supply. This system, ingenious, unobvious, yet immediately comprehensible by the simplest person combined freedom of choice in tins with fair shares. It is typical of a really good administrative discovery.

P.A.Y.E. will be familiar to everyone. It has become the foundation of our own, and many other countries' income tax systems, yet it is only a quarter of a century old. The problem here was the assessment and collection of income tax from many millions of people paying comparatively small amounts. Sending each of them an annual demand created a violent administrative peak at one point in the year. Still more to the point, most of these people were not in the habit of putting a little aside for income tax week by week so as to be able to pay the lump sum demanded at the end of the year; so they found the lump sum difficult to pay.

The device invented was deduction from wages by the employer and payment in monthly lumps to the revenue. But how should the employer know what to deduct for each employee, and how should each employee know—as every taxpayer must know—what he was paying? This is done by giving a code number to every income a tax-payer was likely to have, making allowance in it for all the commoner circumstances affecting tax liability (such as a family), and then working out the tax due on each income. Every taxpayer is then given a code number, and the employer makes the deduction appropriate to that number. This system has not only proved more efficient: by bringing in money all the year round, and not all in a few months at the end of the tax year, it has made the Government less dependent on credit or other forms of taxation.

What have all these discoveries in common? They are all ways of enabling large numbers of people to do business with the government more efficiently. The point lies in the large-ness of the numbers. The construction of something that will work for thousands or millions is at the centre of a civil servant's professional skill. This is why, in modern society, more and more civil servants of any seniority need to have a working knowledge of what a computer can do; though not necessarily of how a computer works. But he will still need linguistic ability, the ability to elicit meaningful answers and explain so that even the least literate can understand. In other words he must be capable of manipulating the form and the explanatory leaflet.

The earliest recorded use of the word 'form' for a printed sheet with blanks for completion, is in Dickens's *Little Dorrit*, published—oddly enough—at almost exactly the time that the modern Civil Service was established in this country. The usefulness of forms goes far beyond administration into sociology, statistics, medicine, economics, demography, commerce, and many operations of everyday life. There are ill- and well-designed forms, and in recent years a great deal of time and expertise has been spent in the Government service on their improvement. A good form is explicit. It never asks for more information than is needed, its questions are unam-biguous and avoid offence. Where a question is complicated it is explained. The layout is uncrowded, and the space allowed for answers is adequate. And the whole thing is not designed only for those who are to complete it. The designer of a form must think also of how his product will fare when bundled into hundreds or thousands and processed by people who have no time to be constantly referring to books of in-structions.

Behind the need for a form lies—however remotely—a de-cision of policy which requires information to be collected in order to administer it. The original sketch of a civil service

—TCSAHW

form therefore originates in a policy-making branch. Even in advising about the policy decision the civil servants concerned will have had some sketch of the forms and procedure in their minds. Once the decision has been taken the form moves into the hands of experts in consistency and layout, and from them back to the policy people. If the form is a new and important one it may, before being approved, be examined by very senior officials and even by ministers. By the time it is printed it will have been looked at not only for the points I have mentioned but as a public relations exercise and a political document.

A good example of a form that crucial planning decisions over several years will depend upon, so that many hours of work in numerous government departments goes into discussing it, is the census questionnaire. It will go to every household in the kingdom. It must be phrased so that everyone whose circumstances are the same will give the same answer. It must be understood by fashion models, Irish labourers, Oxford dons and Lake District shepherds, in the same way. If the questions are ambiguous, decisions will be based on wrong statistics; and decisions based on wrong statistics produce nonsense in administration.

Behind the form is policy; from the yield and practicability of the form, distilled into statistics, policy is constructed. The civil service, in its more senior levels, is sometimes called 'policy making', which sounds rather grand. The fact is that while administration depends on policy, policy cannot exist without administration. If the Civil Service was not concerned with administration, it would have no voice in policy. It is useless for the most talented general to issue orders without either information about the enemy, a map of the neighbourhood, or an army of his own to manoeuvre.

It is true that the civil servant, unlike the scholar or the

scientist, must often make his judgments on incomplete information. Time will not allow him to do otherwise. But nowadays he is more and more concerned with making judgments about the information needed to make better
judgments, and about how to get it. Here is where the new,
expert arms of the Civil Service—the statisticians, economists,
actuaries and scientists, come into the general-purpose administrator's life. He needs their experience and professional
judgment to validate the arrangements he is expert in making: they very often need his to get or organize the information (in the form of statistical surveys and so on) on which
alone their advice can be founded. So one gets the joint
administrative research project, with administrators and experts grouped together. Into such pooling there are three
streams—academic knowledge, awareness of ministerial inten-
tions, and the know-how of collecting and analysing material.

What, when one gets down to it, is 'routine', which is the
way most civil servants are imagined to spend their lives? This
word is often used, especially by officials themselves, as a
synonym for 'unimportant'. 'Merely a routine enquiry, Sir',
says the detective-inspector in an attempt—if it now ever
succeeds, to put the suspect at his ease. There is a clue here.
It is rare for officials to make their enquiries sound important,
even when they are. Sometimes they cannot even know, until
later, how important something they are doing is.

There is another point about routine. One man's crisis is
another man's routine. The bomb disposal squad disarms land
mines, and the ambassador attends diplomatic cocktail parties
as a matter of routine; yet these activities would be far from
routine for, say, a milkman or a filing clerk. In other words
'routine' is the word people use for what their job (any job)
mainly consists of, when they happen to be bored with it.

And being bored depends as much on what sort of a person one is (and how long one has been working without a break) as on the job one is doing. There is probably only one kind of life that does not, in this sense, consist of routine, and that is being a student, since all the time one is discovering something fresh and the whole, so far unexplored, world is spread out in front of one.

It is true that for the most part civil servants go to and from work every day, and that a great deal of their time at work is taken up with reading, writing, and discussion. But even to this there are numerous exceptions. Some civil servants, such as H.M. Inspectors of Schools, are perpetually travelling; some, such as those who work for the National Assistance Board, spend nearly all day listening to, and assessing, the difficulties and troubles of others.

But let me try to describe various kinds of work which may fill the average sort of day for a middling to senior civil servant; and how these tie in with a number of other civil servants senior to him, junior, and on the same level. To make things as simple as possible I will assume that all the kinds of work I am describing happen to concern the same problem— the question of whether to establish a centre for treating and rehabilitating drug addicts. But in fact the letter, the P.Q., and the meeting which follow one upon the other will often be on quite different subjects.

Let us begin with a letter. This is a letter from a doctor who has taken an interest in the problem—has written a paper about it in a medical journal. He has now written enclosing a copy of his article, to his M.P., who has sent it on to the minister with a request for an explanation of what the ministry is doing about it. Like all other letters sent to the minister this one has been tagged on to a distinctive folder by one of the minister's subordinate private secretaries, and sent with a request for a reply within fourteen days. There is now a draft reply on it, typed with a wide margin for amendments, and a minute from the Principal who drew up the reply, explaining the state of the problem, and saying why he thinks this reply is the right one.

This subject is not new to the official now looking at the file. If he has been doing his job he will have noticed the doctor's article already in the press cuttings which come to his desk daily and weekly. He will certainly know the various ways in which rehabilitation of addicts is already being tackled, and other ways of tackling it that are being currently discussed. He will also know the extent of resources which his Ministry is able, at any rate this year, to devote to retraining and rehabilitation, and what claims there are on it.

At this point his own secretary (or personal assistant as she is called in the Civil Service) brings in another folder, containing a Parliamentary Question. It is brightly coloured, so that no one can lose sight of it while it is on a desk. She has looked through all the Assistant Secretary's incoming papers before bringing them in, and entered them in her register, so she knows that this P.Q. is relevant to the letter the Assistant Secretary already has. In the P.Q. the same M.P. has decided not to wait for a reply to his letter. He is asking, for answer within forty-eight hours, what facilities for the treatment of drug addicts exist, what extensions of them are planned, and whether the minister will make a statement.

By common consent replies to Parliamentary Questions are settled exactly beforehand; but the replies to supplementary questions—i.e. the follow-up which the questioner is customarily allowed to put, and often reveals the real object of his question—are impromptu, though they may, of course, have been foreseen. A minister in Parliament is not a witness in a law-court, or the subject of a television interview. He can say as little or as much as he likes, provided that what he says is true.

In framing a draft reply to this question the Assistant Secretary will try to put himself in the position of both his minister and the questioner, but will also use the more detailed knowledge of the subject which he, but neither of them, possesses. His reply will perhaps go something like this:

> I would refer the hon. Gentleman to pages 167 to 170 of my Department's Annual Report for 1965, to which I am not at present in a position to add.

To this will be added a series of notes setting out the current state of the problem and the sort of supplementaries that may be expected, one of which will certainly be:

What about the proposals of Dr X?

To which an answer might be:

> I am aware of this contribution to the problem, which will be included in the studies my Department is making for further methods of progress.

It will now be the business of the Assistant Secretary to carry out this promise. In doing it he will have to lay before the Minister in a report, or what is sometimes called a 'submission', a complete account of the business in all its aspects, as the basis for a decision. This is not the place for personal views. The maker of a submission may feel violently on the subject one way or another, but it is no part of his job to express this. His business is to explain, and so far as possible resolve, the conflicting, even contradictory, hopes and views of others, and the practical possibilities.

To get at these he will probably hold a meeting, summoning the colleagues concerned by letter or minute setting out the questions to be answered as he provisionally sees them. He will use this as a kind of agenda when the meeting assembles. Let us say he summons a doctor from the Ministry of Health, someone from the Children's side of the Home Office, and a finance officer. He himself acts as chairman, and one of his Principals, the one who drafted the original reply to the M.P., acts as secretary. It is his business to take a note.

They sit round a small table kept for the purpose in one corner of the Assistant Secretary's room. By now—it is perhaps a week later—the P.Q. has been answered, and the Assistant Secretary has had the opportunity of a word informally with his immediate superior in the office, his Under-secretary. The discussion will last an hour or so, probably not longer, and the general lines of a submission with points for future action will have emerged. It is now the job of the Principal to work this up into a connected note, perhaps four or five pages long, which he will probably dictate to a shorthand writer or into a dictating machine. If time permits he will circulate what he has written to the people who came to the meeting for their comments and amendments. Sometimes there is no opportunity, and he must just get it right : but he must always send each participant a copy. The ability to reproduce the substance of a meeting with only the briefest notes to guide one comes with practice : the main arguments advanced and the decisions are what is needed, not an account of the actual dialogue. Very often the Chairman will sum up the chief points at the end. The techniques of dictation need to be learned early, otherwise they are often not learned at all. To dictate as briefly as one would write is not easy.

In the course of the days touched on here there will have

been many other activities for the civil servants concerned. But let us turn to something quite different—a day in the life of the manager of a local National Insurance Office. He is a Higher Executive Officer. It will probably begin by a tour round his office—the enquiry counter, the cashier's desk, the correspondence section, and the office where individual payments of benefit are being calculated. In his own office, when he gets there, is a P.Q. asking how many industrially disabled people there were in his area during each of the last five years. He arranges to get it answered from his registers and then (it is now 11 o'clock) goes through the rest of his correspondence, which he completes in time for a lunch with the local Chamber of Commerce, where he gives a short talk about recent changes in the rules for unemployment benefit.

After lunch he is told that a sudden and serious accident has happened at the local coal mine. Several men have been killed, more have been hurt, some are still trapped. He has to do two things immediately: find out all the details he can so that, sympathetically but at once, cash help can be given to the families who have suffered. For this he will probably have to make special staff arrangements, and get in touch with both the mine management and the local miners' lodge. He must also send an immediate report of what he has learned and the steps he has taken to his headquarters. The press and the broadcasting networks will already be asking about his Ministry's action. Later he will send more detailed reports.

I agree that this last emergency is not in any sense 'routine'; but crises, though not usually so tragic as this, occur very often in civil service work. The civil servant must react quickly to these crises in his specialized way, contributing what he is qualified to offer.

For most civil servants the crisis does not present itself as an explosion or an epidemic. It make take the form, at first of a piece of paper or a telephone call very much like hundreds of others. One is not necessarily told that a particular matter is urgent. It is part of a civil servant's professional skill to smell urgency when he meets it, and give it the immediate priority it deserves. It may not bear the bright colours of a P.Q. file or the glamour of a secret envelope, or even a red priority flag. The room in which the civil servant is sitting is just the same as it was before he took up this particular thing and realized its importance; and moved out of routine into a piece of critical business.

CHAPTER VIII

ATMOSPHERE AND MANNERS

THE DETAILS OF how people in a profession behave make them more real and comprehensible. They become life-size. These small habits vary a bit from one department to another, and what I have to say will not be true of everyone or everybody. Indeed one of the things one notices if one changes one's department is the number of small differences of atmosphere and style. When a new department is formed by drafting in civil servants from perhaps two or three older ones, the streams of habit tend to run side by side for a year or so, until one of them gradually predominates. Some departments, for instance, such as the Treasury, file each paper about a given subject below the last so that the file can be read continuously like a book. Others file letters and memoranda on the right of the folder, and on the left the minutes commenting on each. Others again arrange their files so that the latest paper is always on top, which means that the history has to be read in the reverse order of a book. This chapter is about civil service habits. Some, but not all of these apply more in the London Ministries.

Civil servants are great abbreviators. It used to be the custom—still perhaps is—in some departments, to write 'Lay by' on a file that was no longer needed; but the more usual symbol for this is 'P.A.', standing for 'put away'. 'B.F.', followed by a date or period signifies that the file is to be brought forward to be looked at again, and can be elaborated into such a minute as 'B.F. one month to Mr So and So'. Other hieroglyphics are 'K.I.V.' for 'keep in view', 'O.R.' meaning 'on return' and 'N.F.A.' meaning 'no further action'. So that one can get a minute which is almost in code :

> Mr Jenkins (O.R.)
> We sp. N.F.A. now but pl. K.I.V.
> A.B. 29.4.65

In some Departments there are scores of contractions for longish words and phrases in common use, such as ⊙ for a circular, 'i.p.' for 'insured person'. As a result many minutes on case-files would be virtually unintelligible to a stranger, though the language is pretty quickly acquired, and by using it an officer can get through perhaps half as many routine files again than if he wrote at length on each one. But although 'please' is often contracted, as in my example above, it is rarely omitted, and the one-word minute 'Thankyou' is a very common acknowledgment by a senior for a report on completed action or a piece of information from lower down the line. This is not mere formality. It means the senior has read and agrees with it. In fact these minutes are not unlike the well-known communication between the two Quakers, one writing to the other from America for news about England. His letter ran :

> Friend,
>
> ?

and the reply was,

> Friend,
>
> o

A minute may be a direction or an expression of view, but the choice of language in it is for the civil servant who signs it. The minuting on a file is thus the internal discussion of the problem, and is distinct from the memoranda, notes, and letters which represent the department's corporate efforts at each stage. With a memorandum the draft will be opened and then passed round and up the office. Successive alterations and corrections and amplifications and deletions get made until it emerges in a fair copy as the expression of the whole department's views and experience. The scanning of drafts, and the ability to make the minimum alteration required to bring them more exactly into line with the wider horizon of a more senior official without wasting work already done, is an art learned by seeing how a file has developed after it has returned to the man who opened the original draft.

The deletion of words 'put up' by a subordinate, and the substitution of others is an accepted part of civil service life. But it is very rare for a whole draft to be discarded, if the writer has any experience. An experienced and courteous superior who finds himself in total disagreement will more commonly write what he describes as an alternative draft and send it forward saying he prefers it.

Another labour-saving habit is to mark significant passages in the margin of a long document—often with capital letters —and then use these as pegs for comment which will then run, perhaps, 'I agree with X, but doubt if we should proceed now with Y'; or 'Mr So and So, I should be grateful if you would act as at Z of your minute'.

Although there is no offence in simply deleting or altering material put up by one grade to the one above it in a direct chain of responsibility, there is a great deal where a draft is sent by one official to another in a separate area of responsibility for comment from a different point of view. In such cases the comments will either be written out as a separate letter or minute, or, at the very most, pencilled in as tentative changes. This may seem a rather elaborate distinction, but it reflects one of the most important aspects of civil service life: the separation of responsibilities. When one moves from one chain of responsibilities to another, rank and hierarchy cease to count. At a meeting a Principal from one responsibility counts as much as an Under-secretary from another. While meetings and correspondence between civil servants tend to be carried on at 'levels' (that is one rank corresponds with others of equal rank), this is far from being the inflexible rule it once was.

An immense amount of the work of the Civil Service is done by word of mouth, and the conference table in the corner of a civil servant's room is as much his workbench as his desk is. On the whole, civil servants are extremely accessible to one another, and it is unknown to knock on a door in the Civil Service, however grand the official on the other side of it. Those of Assistant Secretary rank and above have secretaries (called 'personal assistants') who usually sit in a connecting room through which visitors come. But even at the highest ranks interruption is always accepted (on the ground that it is never frivolously sought) unless there are other visitors actually in the room or the heat is really on.

'Room', rather than office is the word a civil servant uses for the space he actually occupies. 'Office' tends to be used for the whole building in which he works. He very often calls his desk a 'table', though this oddity, along with the description of a cupboard as a 'press' is gradually dying out. 'Bag' is the way he refers to his rather bulky briefcase, which is easily big enough to hold several fat volumes or the requirements of a country weekend trip.

Sometimes papers are circulated in locked briefcases, known then, for some reason as 'pouches'; but for the circulation of secret and confidential papers from one ministry to another the Civil Service employs what are called, and literally are, boxes. These are of various design, but usually coffin-shaped and about eighteen inches long, with a brass handle set in the top. They are covered in brightly coloured leather, on which is embossed the name of the department. The personal boxes of ministers are covered in scarlet; those of the Treasury and the Cabinet Office are black. Most other departments have green boxes. Each box belongs to a 'suite' controlled by the Private Secretary of the Minister concerned, and the same key will open any box in a given suite. A box will be addressed to a key-holding official by a cardboard label which protrudes between the lid and the box, and is held there by two metal teeth set in the edge of the box, so that when the box is closed the label cannot be changed or removed (short of tearing it off and leaving a tell-tale piece inside the box). When the addressee has dealt with the contents of the box he crosses out his name on the cardboard label, and reverses it so that the other end protrudes to show the name of the office to which the box is to be returned. These boxes appear in pictures going back to the time of the Younger Pitt, and must be among the oldest-fashioned objects in everyday civil service use. Because they are so bulky and conspicuous they are exceptionally secure.

It used to be the custom, and may still be, that a box was made specially for each Royal Commission for the keeping of its confidential papers; and this ultimately became the perquisite—almost the only one in the Civil Service—of the Commission's secretary. Such boxes can still be seen on the side-tables of senior civil servants, rather like the hunting trophies of a gun-room.

In writing to one another officially, civil servants address one another by surnames and sign themselves 'yours sincerely'. This is done even by a civil servant who has never met or dealt with his correspondent before. Titles and distinctions of all sorts, whether earned or inherited, are ignored, except as between the sexes. Thus a woman civil servant writing to a man will begin 'Dear Mr So and So', or 'Dear Sir George', and he, in replying will write 'Dear Miss (or Mrs) So and So' or 'Dear Dame Nancy'. Most civil service correspondence is now in this informal style, and the old kind of letter, known as a 'cocked hat', which began 'Sir, I am directed by . . .' and ended 'I am, Sir, your obedient Servant' is now discontinued as between civil servants. It is also virtually obsolete between the Civil Service and the public, having been finally reduced to ridicule, perhaps, by the letter in this style drafted by a disgruntled civil servant who had been told to draw it up in words of one syllable, and took the instruction literally. He began, 'My Lords have told me', and ended (he was a Treasury Official), 'Should you doubt this you ought to get one of the works on wealth which are to be had at small cost if room can be found in the Vote to buy it.'

Since this is rather a digressive chapter I now turn to the subject of tea, which civil servants are famous for being fond of. So, I suppose, are other desk workers, though for some reason there are no jokes about it. It is undoubtedly the case that civil servants drink a great deal of tea—most of them at least twice a day, once in the middle of the morning, and once in the middle of the afternoon. If a committee is sitting at eleven in the morning or three thirty in the afternoon tea will be brought in, and usually a biscuit as well. The tea comes to be made in various ways. In some offices it is brought round on trolleys, in others it is made by messengers on a private enterprise basis. In some offices the tea in the afternoon is drunk by a branch or division together in the room of one member of the branch. Quite important discussions can take place at these 'tea-clubs', which for a quarter of an

hour or so bring together all the ranks engaged on a particular set of duties. The tea is not supplied by the government, nor is the crockery, except for meetings where visitors
from outside the department are present.

West End leather arm-chair clubs also figure in civil service
life, though possibly to a decreasing extent: canteens improve,
the opportunities for a long lunch-break diminish, and important offices are moved away from Westminster. It is, perhaps
paradoxically, the quiet rather than the company of their
clubs that draws many senior civil servants to them. For a
working lunch the meal is good without being grand, conversation can be heard at one's own table (but not at the next)
and it is all fairly cheap—civil servants, of course, have no
allowance for this sort of purpose. But the solitary luncher,
away from the telephone and the pressure, looking at the
weeklies, is a very common sight in the clubs most frequented
by civil servants, and it is probably for this quiet interval
that many of them cling to membership of the Pall Mall
palaces. On the whole those who belong to clubs tend to
congregate in three or four where the membership is professional rather than smart: the Social Service Departments
at the Oxford and Cambridge; the Revenue Departments and
the Treasury at the Reform. But it does not matter now, if it
ever did, to a civil servant's prospects, whether he belongs to
a club or not.

It is comparatively uncommon, indeed, for civil servants to
take business lunches, either with one another or with people
outside the service. Of course they often discuss business over
their lunches in canteens and messes, but the more elaborate
affair at which some proposition is hatched is not part of the
ordinary method of work. Perhaps this is because civil servants are always wary about being talked into anything while
they are accepting hospitality; perhaps it is because they have

to pay themselves for what they eat. The fact remains that when two civil servants lunch out together their object is mainly social—they may be old friends anyway, or new colleagues who want to get to know one another better. In either case they will probably talk a good deal of shop, but shop is not the same thing as business.

The office festivities of civil servants are very much like those of other office workers. They celebrate Christmas at a series of Branch and Divisional parties that start early in December. A colleague transferring elsewhere, or a woman colleague getting married, are always good for a party, and a retirement is the occasion for a solemn assembly, with speeches and a presentation. I have heard some remarkably good speeches on retirement from men I would never have imagined as orators. Speeches charged, very often, with real emotion and much wisdom.

Many are the stories told on these occasions by older civil servants about how the service has grown less formal since they first joined it; and I sometimes think that the public picture of the Civil Service, like its picture of prisons and schools, is subject to a time-lag of fifty years or so. Convicts do not wear broad arrows, schoolmasters rarely wear gowns and never mortar-boards. But they are very often drawn in these costumes. The civil servant does not wear a stick-up collar, and few pinstripes are seen in Whitehall today. It is much more likely that the newcomer will be puzzled by an informality and lack of apparent rules, than that he will be oppressed by stiffness and stuffiness. He will not, for instance, know how to address his superiors. 'Sir' is certainly not right, and although Christian names come pretty fast, they do not come at once. At meetings it is easier, because surnames are still usual, except for Secretaries and Deputy Secretaries, who are addressed by the names of their jobs, like clergymen.

So far I have been trying to sketch details which are pretty well common to the service as a whole. But as I began by saying each department has a slightly different atmosphere derived partly from the sort of business it does, partly from the outlook of its most senior officers, partly from history, and partly as a result of the building it occupies. A building can be terribly important in setting the style of its inhabitants. The Treasury, with its vast corridors, some of them describing impressive circles round courtyards, and vaulted in a slightly cloistral manner, is a bit like an aquarium. The rooms are high, the furniture, much of it, Victorian. The Home Office also has high rooms and Victorian furniture, but the pavements of the book-lined corridors are tesselated, with occasional show-cases containing medals and trophies. The general effect is more that of a swimming bath. There are plans for both these interesting but obsolete and wasteful buildings to disappear. The Ministry of Defence has a huge entrance hall with elaborate light-metal doors and some modern statuary. The corridors have a sleek, efficient air about them, and the lifts (unlike those of the Treasury, which are tiny, with varnished wooden doors) are automatic, with flickering lights and chiming bells.

The Board of Inland Revenue, with some smaller partners, occupies Somerset House, which was built towards the end of the eighteenth century under an Act of Parliament, specifically to house the then baby-sized Civil Service. As a result the Registrar General, who is responsible for the census, has one of the most beautiful ceilings in London to look at; so have the Commissioners of Inland Revenue when they assemble in their Board Room. The Department of Education and Science, on the other hand, though it has a very good address in Mayfair, occupies an extremely poky building, fortified during the last war on its ground floors for some reason, and with entrances which are very difficult to find. The Ministry of Labour, another Department with a very good address (St James's Square) is rather similar.

The Ministry of Health has a skyscraper at the Elephant and Castle, from the top of which the Permanent Secretary, in his pent-house office, can survey a new London rising from the debris of the old. A few offices—notably the Customs and the National Assistance Board—are in or very near the City. Only two other large ones, apart from the Ministry of Health, are south of the river. One is the Department responsible for all public buildings, the Ministry of Public Building and Works. It houses itself in what must be one of the ugliest blocks in England, a vast squat pile crouching just on the south side of Lambeth Bridge. The other is the Ministry of Transport.

The most gracious of all the Whitehall offices is undoubtedly Dover House, where the London end of the Scottish Office is established. Since the numbers are small, and there is a large proportion of ministers and senior officials among them, this former town house of the Earls of Dover, backing on to the House Guards parade from Whitehall is exactly right though unusual. But the oddest building in the Whitehall complex is probably the ramshackle but rather charming row known as Richmond Terrace, whose eight former town houses have been knocked into a single labyrinth of twisting passages and oddly shaped rooms. These have housed all sorts of offices in their time—the Reconstruction Secretariat that worked on the Beveridge Social Security Scheme, various parts of the Treasury, the Office of the Minister for Science, and now portions of the Department of Education and Science.

A civil servant will have many removals in his career. His effects will be packed up (some departments use hampers, others cardboard boxes) and for a day or two he will exist in chaos, unable to find files or colleagues, cut off from the telephone, dusty and unhappy. But the interruption is brief. Very quickly the basic tools of his trade—table, chair, pen, paper, and phone, take shape and he is transacting public business again. The real atmosphere in the air of all public offices is one of continuity, of a ceaseless flow which will not end with an individual or a building.

CHAPTER IX

OUT OF THE OFFICE

GOING ABROAD AND going home are two things that everyone who works likes to do. For the civil servant there is a strong contrast between the two. When he goes abroad on a job he is on duty pretty well all the time, whether he is at the conference table or an evening party. When he goes home from the office—allowing for the fact that he may take a bag of work or a headful of revolving ideas away with him—he can if he wishes close the doors of his private life completely behind him.

Even in the home-based Civil Service there is now a good deal of work abroad. Some departments have a network of overseas posts. The Board of Trade maintains Trade Commissioner offices in most major countries in the world, to foster British commerce. Most administrative officials in that department can expect to serve a three-year 'tour' at one of these posts, where some executives and clericals are also required. The Ministry of Labour has a number of Labour Attachés abroad who report on industrial relations in the countries where they are stationed, and the Department of Education and Science has a similar corps of Scientific Attachés, who are drawn from the Scientific Civil Service. The Treasury also has several permanent stations abroad.

Often the overseas work of home ministries is concerned with the various international agencies: the Treasury men abroad, for instance, are delegates to standing international finance bodies such as the International Monetary Fund. The

Ministry of Labour is concerned with the International Labour Organization; the Ministry of Overseas Development with U.N.E.S.C.O. and the Food and Agriculture Organization; the Ministry of Health with the World Health Organization. These bodies, of course, need temporary delegations on particular subjects, as well as permanent delegates.

For as a permanent delegate, during a tour of, say, three years, life is not unlike life in the Diplomatic Service, with which, of course, one works closely. One sets up house, brings one's family, and becomes generally established in the British community wherever one happens to be. The temporary visit overseas is rather different. There are some specialists even in visiting, but often an expert has to sandwich one visit lasting two or three days into a year of home-based work.

There are a great many reasons for sending officials abroad, and I doubt if there is a single major department that does not sometimes need to do so. I will give some examples in a moment. But I have never come across a case where a great deal of work was not expected in return for the fare. Travel broadens experience, and one of the reasons for sending an official abroad may be to enable him to learn how other people tackle a problem he is faced with in England. We are much more conscious than we used to be that we can learn from foreigners. There are even a certain number of overseas fellowships for which civil servants can compete, giving a year's study leave in the United States or some other countries. But on the whole, although civil servants usually go abroad with a slight feeling of guilt at being away from their desks, and the words 'swanning about' are heard from time to time, the day abroad is packed fuller than the day at the office. Even more to the point, as I have said above, is the fact that when one is abroad officially one is never completely off duty.

A very common reason for a foreign visit is to find out facts at first hand. This is probably the most satisfying kind of visit. It may be in Scandinavia, or it may be in Italy : one is making contact with people doing a similar job and finding out how they tackle it in its different context. Difficulties that seem enormous in England may seem quite trivial to one's overseas opposite number, and things we find easy may seem to him impossible. This fact-finding work is not merely educational. Often it is combined with another reason for going abroad : negotiation. Before one can negotiate between two systems, the representatives of each must understand the situation of the other.

At any moment of time there are hundreds of international negotiations going on in Europe alone. Most of them are not about peace and war, but concern much more commonplace things such as the terms on which visitors from one country can rely on another country's welfare services; or international telephone wires; or the control of infectious diseases; or collaboration in science and technology; or customs duties; or how far one country is willing to forego taxing someone on income already taxed in another country. All negotiations of this kind must be carried on by administrators who really know the system in their own countries, whether it be National Insurance, the Telephone Service, Port Health, Government Science, Customs, or Income Tax. The time has long passed when this sort of work could be done by professional diplomatists. They are now primarily concerned with what such negotiations mean for international relationships in general, and they come in at the end if there is an agreement to be signed by the Governments of the countries involved. But the actual contents and text of an agreement is for the experts from the ministry that understand the subject.

So there are in Europe, and in the world as a whole, gradually growing up, international groups of specialist officials on nearly every governmental subject. They know one another and one anothers' systems. Just as there is a republic of music and a republic of letters, there are smaller, less picturesque republics of telecommunications, police, pest control, and the suppression of drug trafficking.

Many of these contacts are what is called in the jargon 'bilateral' : that is, two sided. Many more are multilateral, bringing in a number of nations. Multilateral agreements are settled at conferences which are either specially convened or sponsored by one of the international organizations, which cover a great many subjects, from refrigeration to whale hunting and the exploration of space.

The typical conference does not last long—perhaps three or four days. It may or may not aim at producing a new international agreement in a formal sense, but readiness even to go on studying a question is very often a form of agreement. If the conference is a large gathering, like the annual conference of the I.L.O. at Geneva, or of U.N.E.S.C.O. in Paris, the full body may meet only for an opening and a closing session. The main work will be done by committees, whose resolutions will be put to the full conference for adoption. Outside the Committees informal discussions will be going on, and these will often be carried into the evening parties which are usually given. A good deal of the actual writing has to be done in hotel bedrooms late at night. This illustrates what I mean in saying that one is rarely off duty on these occasions.

For a major negotiation, such as the negotiation for the British entry into the Common Market a few years ago, a special organization may well be created, both in the field (in the case of the Common Market this was at Brussels) and in Whitehall. This strong 'home' committee of officials, served by an ad hoc secretariat will keep all the government departments concerned in touch with one another and with the delegation abroad. The people concerned, from the senior officials down to the clerical officers and typists, will be specially detached from their normal jobs for the purpose, and the detachment may last several months.

Another, rather different reason for travelling is to give expert advice to a foreign or commonwealth government. This is a major part of the work of the Ministry of Overseas Development, whose advice is on many different topics—locusts, bilharzia, how to set up a civil service commission, a post office savings bank, or an old age pensions scheme. The expert operates here on his own as a professional man. He may be a scientist, or a doctor, or a general administrator. He is not negotiating or selling anything, but offers his experience and skill as a British official to the overseas government. I knew a silver-haired deputy accountant general once who completely overhauled the financial system of a South American republic.

Private office staff are often called on to travel with their minister abroad. The reason why they go is often not fully understood. The private secretary who goes with a minister is, of course, responsible for the travel arrangements themselves, for the cars meeting trains or aircraft, for the minister's engagement book while on tour, for contact with British officials on the spot. But he is also the link by which the minister, if he is to be away for any length of time, keeps in touch with urgent affairs at home. The work of the office must go on, and it is sometimes necessary to run what amounts to a small travelling office—an extension of the minister's private office in London, to deal with this.

It seems to me likely that in coming years the sorts of

international work I have been describing will develop further. Just as the Whitehall Ministries have been drawn together by the way their problems overlap, and the different kinds of specialists find themselves sitting side by side, so the nations are drawn together by the complex problems that affect them all. This does not mean that every civil servant can expect to go abroad in future, but rather more will do so than in the past.

Most countries use their diplomatic and international contacts as a kind of shop window, and there is still a certain amount of tinsel in international meetings. It is rather like air travel. One is treated more formally than if one were travelling by bus. So men who at home lead quiet and even modest lives may temporarily find themselves in surroundings which are traditional for ambassadors and their staffs. There is still a floweriness and formality between nations that is absent from ordinary civil service work. But the experienced negotiator will often get beneath these skins. The less experienced should be careful not to be carried away by it. There are two useful rules: never try to negotiate in a foreign language, however well you think you speak it; and never enter into competition with Bulgarians in the drinking of vodka, however genially the offer is made.

Most civil servants have left their offices by six in the evening. Some stay till seven. The silence of the telephone and the absence of visitors may tempt a few to tackle a piece of work needing real concentration and stay till eight. A good deal of work—most of it reading matter—is taken home by the more senior. But the office does not reach out into the domestic and private lives of civil servants, as some private companies in America are said to do. And although the atmosphere varies from department to department, there is on the whole none of that enforced 'togetherness' which some occupations have. There is much to take part in, but failure to take part is no sin. Social life—even the organized social life of the office—has very little to do with office life.

All Departments have what is called a Social and Sports Council, in which the innumerable 'club' activities of the staff are organized. With so many people it is possible to have a tremendous range of these, from rugby football and ju-jitsu to chess and madrigals. Many Departments have an elaborate sports day, with cups and shields run and jumped and even shot for; and there is interdepartmental sport as well. The interdepartmental chess championship is, as might be expected, of a high standard. But a great many civil servants take their pleasures quite independently, and come across colleagues with surprise when off duty.

Among the many recreations of civil servants there are two which, somehow, are characteristic. One is music. Choral and instrumental music seems to make a great appeal to officials, especially those of the Treasury and the Board of Trade, who both have notable choirs. But I knew a man in the Ministry of Pensions who was an oracle on the subject of insurability by day, and one of the leading English experts on the madrigal by night. There is something in music which at the same time contrasts with the work civil servants have to do, and satisfies the kind of mind that is able to do civil service work. It brings both relief and satisfaction.

The other is gardening. In spring the sombre porches of the Treasury in Great George Street are ablaze with oblong boxes of bedding plants. This is the stock of the Treasury Horticultural Society for sale, and in the lunch-hour the place resembles a market. In June and July many ministry basements are filled with prize beans and delicate arrangements of herbs in tiny vases, for the annual competition. One civil servant I know has written a best-seller about roses; another used to grow his own tobacco and bury his worn-out clothes to improve the texture of his soil. Five acres was the area cultivated by the Permanent Secretary of a department in which I once served. He specialized in sweet peas and kept himself in vegetables. He was seen at least once slipping into the office with a sack of seed potatoes over his shoulder.

There are, of course, civil servants who see a lot of each other out of the office; and it is a feature of these friendships that friends can have been on two opposite sides of an official argument in which one has been worsted, and yet display no scars of wounded pride or pique. Departmental arguments can be heated and bitterly prolonged, but they are professional. It is not often that one contestant bears the other a grudge. They know that fate may have them fighting from opposite corners in the next match.

But on the whole civil servants do not talk much about business, even to one another, when they meet out of the office. It is part of the detachment which goes with the profession. This does not mean that a civil servant does not sometimes have warm views on all kinds of issues—political, social, and moral. Quite the opposite. He is able to do so by confining them to his private life, and excluding them from his official acts. Those acts do not, of course, necessarily conform with what he thinks his superiors would like to hear—the advice he gives must be the product of his own judgment; but equally they must not be biased by his personal inclinations, feelings, or prejudices. This, much more than any rules imposed from above, is the discipline of the Civil Service.

A few words should be said about honours. The subject is often misunderstood. Until fairly recent times honours were given primarily for service to the state—whether this service was political, military, or official. A tradition grew up that in the public services a certain seniority in a certain rank carried a certain honour. Gradually the principle on which honours are given has changed and the emphasis is now on service to society as a whole, not just to the apparatus of the state. The two are different, though perhaps not so clearly separate as they once were. But the practical effect is that since honours must be limited if they are to be valued, and the limited number must be spread over a far wider field, the honours for the domestic civil service are far fewer. They are in consequence more highly valued.

The more modest honours—I.S.O., M.B.E., B.E.M.—especially are now marks either of some piece of outstanding work or of exceptionally long meritorious service. I do not suppose that anyone today is tempted to join the Civil Service by the prospect of letters after his name. But if there are any such, they are under a wholly false impression, which should at once be discarded.

I have tried to show that it is not easy to follow the civil servant into private life. He is not gregarious in any very obvious way. There are no local civil service circles as there are miners' lodges or branches of the B.M.A. His private world is very much what he wishes to make of it in his own neighbourhood; and even his wife is unlikely to be troubled with accounts of what old so and so said in the office or how her husband triumphed or would have triumphed if things had gone just a little differently. A wise civil servant has something in his life besides his official work on which to engage himself.

CHAPTER X

CONCLUSION: CREDITS AND DEBITS

THIS CHAPTER IS an attempt to list the qualities that go to make a happy, reasonably successful civil servant; and the disadvantages that one must accept, along with the many advantages, if one decides to take up civil service life. The two—credits and debits—go together, because to some kinds of personality the disadvantages of civil service life are not really disadvantages at all. To others they are, or may be frustrations, so it is just as well to take them into account in advance. Of course there is room for all kinds of character in the Civil Service, from the buccaneer to the curate, so I am not trying to describe a particular type or pattern of character in what follows. I have merely touched on some features one needs. Many of them can be acquired by habit.

I would rate companionableness very high. In the course of almost any civil service career one has to work intimately, often under conditions of difficulty and pressure, with all kinds of people. And when I say 'work with' I mean not only as a member of a team on a specific project, but with civil servants outside one's own team, whose interest in one's problem may not be at all the same as one's own. To differ amicably, while keeping to one's viewpoint and striving to find the reconciling answer, is most important. Whatever kind of work is in hand, it often has to be carried forward in ways which formal and stiff people find troublesome; the professional techniques often are, and must be, brought to bear in short meetings of a few people—hardly more than conversations—or in brief notes, rather than in elaborate committees and long, solemn memoranda.

Equal in importance with companionableness I would put adaptability of mind. This comes in in many ways. Civil servants with a broad span of responsibility very rarely have a day free from interruptions, during which they can concentrate on one particular problem. The file for next week has to be laid aside in favour of the file for tomorrow; and that in turn for the file demanded before lunch. Colleagues will come in unheralded and expect to have their business attended to—for it is understood that except for very senior officials indeed formal appointments do not need to be made if there is something urgent to discuss. If it is not visitors, it is the telephone. So for many officials, the mind must be capable of constant switching from one subject to another, and going into top gear at once.

There is another, deeper reason, for saying flexibility of mind is important for civil servants. Very often, whether he likes it or not, a civil servant has to change his way of thinking about a problem. After long effort and study he may have arrived at what he regards as a correct solution : it fits in every respect; he has convinced his senior colleagues and his opposite numbers in other departments; he sees in his mind's eye exactly how the thing should be done. Then something happens—a political change, a financial crisis, a decision on some totally different question—which has the unexpected effect of blocking his favoured plan. He is back at his desk with orders to find another solution.

The experienced civil servant will therefore avoid deep personal commitment to one particular solution, however good it seems. He will always foresee, in supporting the solution he thinks best, that some other possibilities are also there. Circumstances change suddenly, the gentlemen in Whitehall and public opinion do not always see eye to eye, what seems second best to the expert may none the less seem better to other people because it is more easily understood, because it can be done more quickly, or for a thousand other reasons : and it is with other people's business, not his own, that the civil servant is always concerned. Decisions cannot be put off until all obstacles to perfection have been removed, and the temporary, the transitional, the highest common factor of agreement at any one time, is something the civil servant often has to work with. As we all know, the highest common factor of a set of large figures is often a very small quantity indeed.

This does not mean that intellectual convictions have to be changed; but that the mind must be capable of detaching itself from them, and working out how best to do what may well seem second best. The only consolation is that since there is almost never finality in any serious question, the wheel may once again turn towards the solution that had to be discarded for the time being. But just because there is finality so rarely, the civil servant should beware of getting into a position that depends on it.

Flexibility of mind, I suppose, is very close to patience, which is another of the civil service virtues. Impatience, of course, is also a virtue when it is directed against abuses, inefficiency, or wrongdoing. But patience—in the sense I am using the word—does not mean simply putting up with the undesirable. It is willingness to look at all sides of a thing, and not just at one of them; to try to worry some kind of sense out of an ill-written letter from an obscure old-age pensioner; to make sure that the arrangements he is making for members of the public to do something deal not only with the obvious cases, but are really watertight, so that someone born of stateless parents on a Japanese ship in Panamanian territorial waters knows how they apply to him. Above all patience is putting up with inevitable frustrations and not losing nerve, temper, or sense of purpose.

Which brings one, naturally, to persistence. It is, if you like, the other side of the medal from the flexibility just discussed. But not its opposite. The two go together, and can always be combined. The civil servant needs to be able to keep up pressure on himself, his subordinates if he has any, his colleagues and his superiors; and in trying to reconcile the various bits of each puzzle he is set, he must judge, and then observe, whatever limits of discretion that have been given to him. Sometimes these are not laid down from above, but are only implied, so that judgment on one's sticking point —the point one cannot concede without authority from above—becomes very important. It may well be that a civil servant, in a tough negotiation, will feel that a concession to the other man's point of view ought to be made, but he must not be flattered or pressurized into making it if he judges that it would affect others, not so far consulted, besides himself. He will break off the negotiation, and then, perhaps advise his superior or the colleague who is affected that the point ought to be given away.

Persistence counts in another way too. Whatever parcel of work or 'seat' has been given him, he should be constantly exploring its possibilities and its frontiers. If possible he should read round it, keep abreast of the current pamphlet literature about it, slant the reading of his newspaper with his particular subject in mind. This goes a good deal further than just noting items on one's subject directly. Take a civil servant concerned with the control of the school building programme. He will probably not be interested in newspaper accounts of the actual programme when it is announced. He knew that already, and his main interest in this will be its treatment in the press, and in any inaccuracies and misunderstandings

5—TCSAHW

that creep in. He is much more interested, say, in a financial article which forecasts that there is going to be a change in the price of cement, or a well worked out attack on the current birth-rate forecasts by a professor of demography.

The pedestrian virtues of accuracy and orderliness are also very necessary for civil servants. Most new recruits to the service get a kind of hardening course in accuracy from their first superiors, who point out slips and mistakes which do not, perhaps, matter much in themselves, with the same kind of purpose as a drill-sergeant, though not in the same manner. But it is a very common practice for more senior civil servants, when they have written something, to ask a subordinate who knows the subject in greater detail than they do, to read it through and comment 'on correctness' before it is sent forward. Thus a Principal may find himself going bail for the accuracy, though not the judgments, in a submission made by his Permanent Secretary to the Minister.

It is difficult to think of a profession in which accuracy is not important; but in the Civil Service an error can only be put right, quite often, by a public correction and apology, which is very rightly taken as a reflection on the efficiency of the whole organization. A wrong figure, a mistaken fact, or even a misfiled paper, can have results out of all proportion to the size of the mistake or the rank of the person who actually made it. One need not be a particularly precise person if one is considering a civil service career; but one has to be willing to accept the habit of checking every way. It is built into the civil service system at every stage to correct the slips that even the most careful commit, before they can do any harm.

Incorruptibility is not really a virtue at all, but something needs to be said about it. Most organizations expect their employees to be honest and to serve them faithfully. But the public service goes rather further than this. It expects not only that its employees should be honest and faithful, but that they should avoid putting themselves into any situation where their private interest and their public duty might conflict. Many civil servants, including quite humble ones, come to know things which they could turn to advantage in their private lives by, so to speak, stealing a march on the rest of society. For a civil servant to do this would be corrupt. Another example is the chance which brings the case of a personal friend to a civil servant's desk, to be dealt with by him officially. Now there is nothing in civil service morality that prevents one telling a friend, as such, where he stands officially, whom he should see or write to, even how he should explain his case. But this is quite different from helping a friend in a way which enables him to get something other people in the same position would not get, simply because he happens to be on friendly terms with a civil servant. This is corrupt. The usual practice, when faced with an official case involving a personal friend—which may of course turn up quite innocently—is to ask that it should be dealt with by a colleague.

The personal integrity expected of a civil servant—which goes so far that it would be considered wrong to write a personal letter to a friend outside the public service on official notepaper—is demanded by the public itself, rather than the Department in which he serves. While, generally speaking, civil servants are not more moral than other men, their professional integrity has to be positive : it is not just a question of keeping within rules laid down. It is not enough for a civil servant to say 'there is no rule against my doing this, and therefore it is all right'. One has to go further and say, 'If this had to be justified to an unsympathetic audience, would they approve?' For everything a civil servant does which has any relation to his work at all—and this extends well beyond what he does at his desk—can come before such an audience, even though it is often the department, not the individual civil servant, who has to answer.

I am emphasizing this, even though it may seem superfluous to most people, and hypocritical to some. But I make no apology, because quite apart from the fact that everyone wants to have an honest public service, the almost puritan tradition about corruption is responsible for two important features of civil service life as a whole. The first is the extent to which civil servants can rely on one another. Words given between civil servants are rarely broken (which of course makes civil servants cautious about giving their words); statements are always true—which sometimes makes them seem skimpy, tortuous, or evasive, since they must not on any account be false. But even more important, the known professional conscience of the Civil Service has great constitutional significance. Because it is known to exist, there is a whole range of activities which governments would find it difficult to undertake, even if they were inclined to them : not political acts in the ordinary sense, which many people may disagree with, but which a civil servant is professionally bound to carry out; but acts which run counter to law, financial integrity, or personal honesty.

Next in this catalogue of virtues comes discretion. Here again, I suppose discretion is a good thing in itself, and all business needs it, rather as all eggs need salt. But because the business of a civil servant is the business of the public, and not his own, there is perhaps more temptation to make an impression by talking about it, and indiscretion can do correspondingly wider damage. I am not here thinking only about great affairs of state, secret weapons, and such like, though knowledge of these has to come to lesser civil servants as well as highly placed ones : the Budget has to be typed, the minutes of cabinets have to be duplicated and filed. But in this sort of thing the need for discretion is perfectly obvious, and there are arrangements, on which I shall touch later on, for enforcing it.

One needs more homely but less obvious examples of how discretion matters in the civil service. Take the Ministry of Pensions and National Insurance, which is in essence a vast organization for collecting contributions at the right rates and times from the people who ought to pay them, and paying benefits promptly to the people to whom they are due. But to do this the Ministry must maintain a complete record of the names, addresses, ages, diseases, marriages and divorces of all the people who are insured : that is, of practically everyone in this country. These simple little personal particulars matter to people, for all kinds of reasons, and they are compelled by law to let the government know them—or at least they must give them if they are to get the benefits to which they are entitled. A person's age may matter (or he may think it matters) very much in getting or keeping a job. The illness a person has may well be something they want to keep to themselves; all kinds of people, for the best of reasons, may want to know someone's address, and that someone may have equally good reasons for not wanting them to know it.

The Ministry will not, of course, let anyone know this kind of personal information without the permission of the person to whom it belongs. The fact that the civil servants employed by the Ministry will not chat or gossip about them is the ultimate guarantee of the confidence between the Ministry and its public. Obviously such chat and gossip, and still more any actual attempt to *publicize* some piece of information— say that someone is suffering from leprosy—is a breach of that confidence. The point is that a civil servant must resign himself to talking comparatively little about the details of his work, even if it is not obviously secret, because it is likely to concern the affairs of individuals which it is necessary for the civil servant to know about, but which are not less private on that account.

Civil servants do from time to time come under pressure—which may be political, but is more usually just social—to give information or say what their view is about something. A view expressed by a civil servant about a professional matter is likely to be equally unfortunate, whether it agrees with, or differs from, his department's official attitude. If it agrees, but the department's view is not yet known, the utterance of the civil servant can turn out to be a 'leak', so that what was to be in his minister's speech on Thursday appears in Wednesday's newspaper. If the department's view is known already, and the civil servant just echoes it, he is liable to sound like a propagandist, and it is no part of his duty to preach the Government's case to his friends. The civil servant who differs from his department in private conversation is obviously put in a ridiculous and embarrassing position.

There is a story of a highly placed civil servant who was asked point blank by a journalist whether such and such a thing was going to be done. The journalist knew that the civil servant knew the answer. The reply he got was, 'Do you really think it would be a good idea to do that?'

Luckily, discretion is an easy virtue to acquire, and it becomes so much part of a civil servant's nature that there is a whole mass of things he does not know consciously except when he is working or thinking about his work—as some civil servants do while gardening or painting their fireplaces. There is a true story about the Budget. Its preparation is, of course, kept to a very small circle. By long tradition the

Principal Private Secretary to the Chancellor of the Exchequer acts as editor of the Budget Statement, and this involves him in a whole series of drafts to be circulated, discussed, amended, and finally reduced to the statement made by the Chancellor in the House of Commons. During the weeks before the Budget the Private Secretary's messenger is constantly carrying round these successive drafts to the people who have to advise on them. And yet, on one occasion, when Budget Day came, this very messenger kept popping into the Private Secretary's room with the latest bulletin about what the Chancellor was saying in the House as it came over the tape, with appropriate comments, just as if it was hot news, having wholly dismissed from his mind the fact that the Private Secretary undoubtedly knew every word of it by heart.

Finally comes clarity of mind. Perhaps I should have put it first. Clarity of mind is not quite the same thing as knowing one's own mind, in other words, decisiveness. Many civil servants have to be decisive in their own spheres if they are to be efficient, but on matters of importance the responsibility for a decision will lie elsewhere. The professional skill required of the civil servant is fundamentally a complete, effective, and unbiased mind which can present issues for discussion or decision. Lack of bias does not mean lack of clarity—'waffle' in civil service slang. It does not mean even, when the analysis is reduced to writing, that it should not point to a conclusion that the writer has reached. It often does, and usually should. After all, each link in an argument is in one sense a conclusion.

But conclusions and analyses are distinguishable. 'Must,' said Queen Elizabeth I to one of her advisers who had been so mistaken as to use the word to her, 'is not a word to be used to Princes.' The Civil Service has taken this lesson very much to heart in its relations with its democratically elected masters. However compelling he may find the arguments, a civil servant will never present his recommendation in such a way that disagreement is impossible.

Having tried to catalogue the qualities a civil servant needs or should try to develop, I shall devote the rest of this chapter to some account of the limitations which these virtues and the rules of the Service impose on him. To some kinds of character these restrictions can matter a good deal—to others hardly at all. It is like the fable of the dog and the wolf in Aesop. The wolf was enthralled by the dog's account of his comfortable well-fed life, until he noticed his collar, and asked why it was worn. When the wolf learned that the dog was sometimes tied up, he decided he preferred starvation in the forest.

What must the servant of the public accept as the price of his salary, his personal security, his pension, and the confidence of society? The restrictions, formally, are not more irksome in themselves than, say, the ethical code of a doctor or the professional etiquette of the Bar; but they may appear to be, because the Civil Service is not, and cannot be, a self-governing profession like medicine or the law. The ultimate sanctions of professional conduct in the Civil Service are imposed and administered by the government itself. There is no General Medical Council, no General Council of the Bar, as custodian of the civil servant's professional standards; nor, really, any such thing as a court martial system like those in the armed services, under which an officer can be formally tried for professional failures as well as for straightforward crimes.

The most familiar restriction, which anyone who reads the newspapers will know about, concerns security. In a sense everything a civil servant comes to know in the course of his duties can be an official secret—that is, something not to be told without authority to anyone who has no business to know it. The Official Secrets Acts—which apply to all citizens, and not just to civil servants—catch the gossip and the sensationalist as well as the spy. But civil servants who are in touch with secrets as most people understand the term are specially investigated, and these enquiries cover their private lives as well as their official behaviour. Thus a civil servant may find that a particular post which he hopes for or expects does not come his way; or he may, because the enquiries are repeated from time to time, find that he is moved to a less sensitive post. In particular no one who is known to be a member of, or actively associated with or in sympathy with, the Communist Party or with Fascist organizations, is employed on secret work. Transfer elsewhere is usually possible : but if it is not, say in the case of a particular kind of electronics engineer, there may be dismissal. Before any such step is taken the civil servant concerned has the right to seek to clear himself before a special tribunal of three advisers who then report to the minister in charge of the department. The civil servant is provided with the evidence which has led to the conclusion that he is not suitable for the work on which he is employed, and can have the help of his Association in presenting his case to the three advisers. But the decision of the minister in charge is final.

Security is one thing, the political neutrality of the Civil Service is another. 'Political neutrality' is not quite the right phrase, because the Civil Service is professionally bound to work its utmost for whatever government is in power, and so is identified with the policy of the party which supports that government in Parliament. But a strong, though invisible line is drawn between the Civil Service and the party machines, and this takes the form of rules against civil servants taking part in party politics. The further removed a civil servant is from the framing of policy or its execution, the smaller is the restriction, and all civil servants do, of course, vote as they please and hold their personal political opinions. A very large part of the service—all the industrials, and grades such as postmen, telephonists, and messengers—is subject only to the rule that a civil servant must resign if he proposes to stand for Parliament. A further large part, comprising the clerical and typing grades, can take part in local government, though if they are engaged in certain kinds of work individual permission from the department is required. The administrative, executive, professional, scientific, and technical grades are not allowed to take part in national political activities, though they may, with permission, take part in local government where this is not organized on national party lines. Both civil servants and politicians are very particular about this. A civil servant must on no account attend a minister at a party conference—not even the minister's private secretary. The minister's official car must not drive him to make a party speech. Still less may a civil servant make a public speech himself, or write a letter to the papers, except as the mouthpiece of his department.

These disabilities are real but accepted because they go with the whole idea of the profession as it has developed in this country. What is perhaps more irksome is that a civil servant can never answer back and justify himself against public criticism, however unreasonable he may think it to be. He may be attacked for signing a letter it was his job to write, or hear his profession or his department run down in ways he believes or knows are wholly untrue or unfair. The various Civil Service Associations do their best to defend the professional reputations of their membership in general. But apart from this the individual civil servant just has to put up with it. However hard he is tried, he must remain silent.

LIST OF GOVERNMENT DEPARTMENTS

Name of Department	*Remarks*
Actuary, Office of the Government	Employs actuaries, executives and clericals allied to Treasury.
Agriculture, Fisheries and Food	Employs all Treasury classes and many specialists, notably vets.
Agriculture for Scotland	Ditto. Located at Edinburgh.
Aviation	Science-based. Employs all Treasury classes, and many scientists.
Charity Commission	Independent of ministers. Staff Administrative, Executive, Legal and Clerical.
County Courts	Executive and Legal. Widely distributed.
Customs and Excise	Administrative, Departmental and Clerical. Widely distributed.
Defence	All Treasury classes. Many scientists. Widely distributed.
Development, Scottish	All Treasury classes
Economic Affairs	All Treasury classes and economists.
Education and Science	All Treasury classes. Scientists. Her Majesty's Inspectors.
Education for Scotland	All Treasury classes. Her Majesty's Inspectors. Located in Edinburgh.
Exchequer and Audit	Mainly Executive.
Export Credits Guarantee	All Treasury classes. Close working with commerce.

Name of Department	*Remarks*
Forestry Commission	Independent of ministers. Widely distributed specialist department.
General Register Office General Register Office (Scotland)	Administrative, Executive and Clerical. Subject to peaks of work. Allied to Health Departments.
Health	All Treasury classes, and doctors and dentists.
Home Office	All Treasury classes, and many specialists.
Home and Health, Scottish	As two preceding. Located in Edinburgh.
Housing and Local Government	All Treasury classes, and many specialists (e.g. planning staff and auditors).
Information, Central Office of	Information Officer class, Executive and Clerical.
Inland Revenue	Administrative, Inspectorate, Executive and Clerical. Widely distributed.
Labour	Administrative, Departmental, Executive, and Clerical, with certain specialists (e.g. Inspectors of Factories). Widely distributed.
Land Registry	Mainly Executive. Widely distributed.
Law Officers Lord Chancellor	Legal and Executive. Small.
National Assistance Board	Administrative (small), Executive and Clerical. Widely distributed.
Ordnance Survey	Specialist
Overseas Development	All Treasury classes, and many specialists.
Pensions and National Insurance	All Treasury classes. Widely distributed.

Name of Department	*Remarks*
Post Office	The largest of all Departments. Employs all classes. Widely distributed.
Power	All Treasury classes.
Public Building and Works	All Treasury classes and many specialists (architects, engineers). Widely distributed.
Stationery Office	Specialist. Allied with Treasury.
Statistical Office, Central	Statisticians and Clerical.
Supreme Court	Legal and Executive.
Technology	All Treasury classes and scientists. Has a provincial network.
Trade	All Treasury classes and certain Departmental classes. Widely distributed. Has many overseas posts.
Transport	All Treasury classes and many specialists.
Treasury	All Treasury classes and some specialists (economists, statisticians, valuers).
Wales	All Treasury classes. Offices in Cardiff and London.

APPENDIX B

ENTRY TO THE CIVIL SERVICE

FULL INFORMATION ABOUT entering the many different branches of the Civil Service can be got from the Civil Service Commission, 23 Savile Row, W.1. The notes which follow are only intended to give the bare bones about entry into a selection of careers at the first rung of the ladder. But there are so many steps across from one ladder to another, or from the middle of a career outside the Civil Service to one inside it, that no tabular presentation could do justice to them. It is particularly important to remember that many recruits to the Civil Service come in on a *temporary* basis, and that the temporary civil servant can compete alongside those who have never been in the Civil Service, for *established* (i.e. permanent) posts. Temporary posts are often, indeed more often than not, filled by the Department concerned, which advertises them. Permanency must be after test by the Civil Service Commission.

Branch of the Service	Conditions	Test
Administrative Class (Assistant Principal)	Age 20–27 inclusive. In effect a good honours degree or dip. tech.	Two methods: Method I: qualifying examination, academic examination, interview. Method II: qualifying examination, tests and interviews, final interview. January and April and (Method II) September each year.
Executive Class (Executive Officer)	Age 17½–23 inclusive. G.C.E. passes in five subjects, including two at Advanced level obtained at same sitting. Degree or dip. tech.	Selection by interview held at frequent intervals.
Tax Inspectorate (Inspector of Taxes)	Age 20–27 inclusive. (a) Degree (not necessarily of honours standard). (b) Good hons. degree or professional accountancy qualification.	(a) As for Administrative Class. (b) Modified version of Administrative Class (Method II) (continuous).
Scientific Officer Class (Scientific Officer)	Age under 29. Good hons. degree or dip. tech. in science, engineering or mathematics.	Selection by interview (continuous).
Experimental Officer Class (Assistant Experimental Officer)	Age 18–27 inclusive. Degree, dip. tech., H.N.C. If under 22, G.C.E. passes in five subjects including two at Advanced level (in science or mathematics) obtained at the same sitting.	Selection by interview. Held in the spring and autumn.
Statistician Class (Assistant Statistician)	Age 20–27 inclusive. Good hons. degree in or including statistics.	Selection by interview in the spring.

Branch of the Service	Conditions	Test
(Cadet Statistician)	Age 20–26 inclusive. Good hons. degree in economics, mathematics or other suitable subjects.	Selection by interview in the spring. Those selected go on to a one year university course leading to a higher qualification in statistics. If they obtain this they are appointed as Assistant Statisticians.
Architects (Basic grade)	Age at least 25. Registered architect.	Selection by interview (continuous).
Information Officer Class (Assistant Information Officer)	Suitable experience. No set age limits.	Selection by interview (quarterly).
Factory Inspectorate (Inspector of Factories)	Age 21–29 inclusive. Degree, dip. tech., or comparable professional qualification: or, if five years suitable experience, at least O.N.C. or Advanced levels.	Selection by interview (continuous).
Economists (Economic Assistant)	Age 20–29 inclusive. Good hons. degree or post-graduate degree in economics or closely related subject.	Selection by interview.
(Cadet Economists)	Age 20–26 inclusive. Degree in economics or any other subject.	Selection by interview. Those selected undertake a one or two year university course in economic subjects. Those who obtain a satisfactory qualification are appointed as Economic Assistants.
Lawyers (Legal Assistant)	Age 24–39 inclusive. Barrister or admitted solicitor.	Selection by interview (continuous).
Engineers (Engineering Cadet)	Age under 26. Good hons. degree or dip. tech. in engineering or physics.	Selection by interview (continuous).
(Basic Grade)	Age 23–35. Full academic requirements of a major institution.	Selection by interview.
Technical and Engineering Draughtsman Classes	Age at least 21. O.N.C. in engineering or closely allied subject.	Selection by interview.

Branch of the Service	Conditions	Test
Probationer Naval Constructor	Age under 27. Good hons. degree in engineering or (with practical experience) naval architecture.	Selection by interview in the spring.
Clerical Class (Clerical Officer)	Age at least 16. Five G.C.E. Ordinary levels including English language.	Selection by interview. Written exam. for those without G.C.E. qualifications.
Scientific Assistant Class (Scientific Assistant)	Age 17–26 inclusive. Four G.C.E. Ordinary levels including English language and either mathematics or science. One year's practical experience.	Selection by interview (continuous).

APPENDIX C

SHORT LIST FOR FURTHER READING

G. A. Campbell (Geo. Duckworth & Son Ltd): *The Civil Service in Britain* (Second Edition 1965).
A good general work.

Civil Service Commission (Stationery Office): *Civil Service Posts for Graduates* (Fourth Edition, 1963).

The Commission also publish booklets on all the major professional people employed in the Civil Service, and on the main Treasury Classes (Administrative, Executive and Clerical).

Estimates Committee (Stationery Office): *Sixth Report, Session 1964–65: Recruitment to the Civil Service.*
The latest of many inquiries into the Civil Service (1965).

H.M. Treasury (Stationery Office): *The Organisation of the Scientific Civil Service* (1965).
A Report by Officials.

The Whitehall Series (Allen & Unwin).
Each volume gives a description of a Department by a civil servant who once presided over it as Permanent Secretary. Most Departments are now covered by this series.